SOULFUL
Minimalism

SOULFUL
Minimalism

20 PRACTICES FOR PASSIONATE LIVING WITH LESS

KAREN ROSE KOBYLKA

Soulful Minimalism

Karen Rose Kobylka

Published by Karen Rose Kobylka, 2024.

While every precaution has been taken in the preparation of this book, the publisher assumes no responsibility for errors or omissions, or for damages resulting from the use of the information contained herein.

SOULFUL MINIMALISM

First edition. September 8, 2024.

Copyright © 2024 Karen Rose Kobylka.

ISBN: 978-1738329335

Written by Karen Rose Kobylka.

Table of Contents

Soulful Minimalism 1
Introduction 4
Chapter One: Living on Less 7
Chapter Two: The Layers of Healing 15
Chapter Three: Power of Forgiveness 25
Chapter Four: Journaling Yourself to Recovery 31
Chapter Five: Mindset Mastery 39
Chapter Six: Declutter and Organize 49
Chapter Seven: Choosing Supportive Relationships 62
Chapter Eight: Finding Your Passion: Your Life's Purpose 70
Chapter Nine: Navigating Your Journey—Goals and Values 76
Chapter Ten: Educate to Elevate - Building a Fulfilling Life 90
Chapter Eleven: Guided Growth: The Power of Mentorship 99
Chapter Twelve: The Path to Spiritual Fulfillment 103
Chapter Thirteen: Raising Your Vibration 108
Chapter Fourteen: Trusting Your Gut - A Guide to Intuition 112
Chapter Fifteen: Gratitude and Appreciation 123
Chapter Sixteen: Nourishment From the Inside Out 128
Chapter Seventeen: Living with Compassion 134
Chapter Eighteen: Soulful Service 139
Chapter Nineteen: Explore Your Creativity 147
Chapter Twenty: Removing Life's Distractions 158
Chapter Twenty-One: Embracing Your Own Unique Life 171
Recommended Reading 177
References 178
Acknowledgements 179
Meet Karen Rose Kobylka 180

To Linda, the richest woman I know. Your spirit, resilience, and joy have inspired this book. Thank you for showing me that true wealth comes from within.

Disclaimer

The author of this book does not provide medical advice or prescribe the use of any techniques as a form of treatment for physical, emotional, or medical problems. The content within this book is intended solely to offer information of a general nature to assist you in your journey. The publisher and author assume no responsibility for your actions based on the information presented in this book. Always consult with a qualified healthcare provider for medical advice and treatment.

KAREN ROSE KOBYLKA

"On a starry night beneath a full moon, you will find your soul dancing among the stars."
— Karen Rose Kobylka

SOULFUL MINIMALISM

"Be brave and embark on your journey of transformation. Here, your soul's purpose will be revealed—the self you've longed to become. This is when your sneakers turn into ruby slippers, and your dirt road leads to a yellow brick road. Embrace the miracle of magic as you grow wings to fly! Take the Soulful Minimalism transformation."
—Karen Rose Kobylka

Introduction

*S*oulful Minimalism embraces simplicity and the joy found in life's essentials. It calls us to align with our true nature and live passionately with less, uncovering the profound beauty in simplicity. This book is your guide to navigating life's journey with a soulful heart and a soul full of purpose.

I have little to show for my 56 years, other than the belongings that fit into the room I rent. After mental illness destroyed my life, I wrote a memoir called *Soul Dance*. To get the full scope of where I have been, I urge you to read that story. It showcases my journey, what I have learned, and why I am the way I am today. It also highlights my gift as a spiritual medium. I channel spirit through the "collective souls" —a collection of consciousness made up of energetic beings and souls that have passed on.

During this time, as I was studying mediumship to advance my skills, I began to mentally unravel and fell into psychosis and mania. When I sought help from my spiritual minister, the church's support failed me. Soon after, they called the police on me, resulting in a charge of criminal harassment. I ended up spending over two months in a psychiatric hospital and a few hours in jail when I went to court for these charges. I was placed on probation for a few years, which significantly lowered my self-esteem, my vibration, and my faith in people. I emotionally shut down and closed myself off from the world.

It took a lot of soul searching to find myself beneath the rubble of destruction life had left me with. Being on a budget, I didn't have the option of going to counseling, as even the discounted rates were unaffordable on my disability income, which barely covers rent and groceries. So, I did the best I could—I journaled. Journaling led me to write *Soul Dance: A Medium's Triumph over Bipolar, Mania, Psychosis, and Betrayal*.

You see, when I was studying mediumship with world-renowned mediums, I owned a beauty empire with 16 thriving salons. When mental illness crept in, I lost everything, leaving me penniless and on welfare, and eventually, disability. I had to do a lot of soul searching to get to where I am today. I was also homeless for a short time but was blessed to find living arrangements before ending up on the street.

SOULFUL MINIMALISM

I live a very modest life on government disability due to bipolar disorder. With an income of $1,535.00 per month and a rent of $900, I am left with $80 a week for groceries and spending money after paying my bills. Occasionally, I receive a bit of extra income, which I use for small indulgences like lunch with friends.

Writing this book has been a journey of self-healing, discovery, and understanding how I got here. After moving from my previous rented room to my current space, which includes a office for writing, I realized how truly happy I am. Despite having no savings or retirement fund, I feel blessed beyond measure.

It's just me against the world — or rather, with the world. I hold no animosity towards those who have tried to harm me; I have forgiven and moved on. This forgiveness is just one aspect of what it took to uncover my formula for leading a passionate life with less.

When I first decided to write this book, I was sitting in my rented room, having a glass of white wine. I let my "collective souls" — the spirits I channel — guide and inspire me, helping me discover the joyous adventure of creating a new book. One day, while in a "Zen" state, the ideas for this book came pouring out of me.

Soulful Minimalism is a book designed to inspire those living a modest life or facing financial or other challenges, to lead their best lives. I want to help you find the silver linings in your journey, much like I have. Having lived on both sides of the fence, I can tell you that the impoverished side is just as valuable as the other. It's all about what you make of it.

I understand that life can be difficult. With bipolar disorder, I navigate deep highs and lows, making life particularly challenging. It is in these challenges that we find new perspective. When I discovered I had bipolar disorder, it initially destroyed my life. Yet, through this destruction, I found joy. Without knowing the depths of the lows, the heights of the highs would hold no meaning.

While I may not have all the answers, I do have a formula for leading a fulfilling, simple life. This formula is broken down into 20 chapters, each focusing on a different aspect of passionate living with less. Through personal stories, practical advice, and reflective exercises, each chapter will guide you on a journey to find joy and purpose in simplicity.

In this book, you will discover:

1. How to embrace minimalism and find freedom in simplicity.
2. Ways to cultivate a positive mindset despite financial constraints.
3. Strategies for keeping faith when times are tough.
4. Tips for creating a nurturing and inspiring living space, no matter how small.
5. The importance of self-care and maintaining mental health.
6. How to build meaningful relationships and a supportive community.
7. Finding and pursuing passions and hobbies that enrich your life.

And much more.

Soulful Minimalism is a practical guide interwoven with personal experiences. By the end of this book, my hope is that you will see the value in every aspect of your journey and find the courage to dance through life, no matter your circumstances.

"The Moon is magic for the soul and light for the senses."
—Unknown Author

Chapter One: Living on Less

Welcome to *Soulful Minimalism*, where you will discover the art of passionate living with less. This book is based on my formula to help you lead a passionate life, even when finances are not abundant. This morning, I did something I rarely do—I logged onto social media. There, I stumbled upon an interview with a famous actor who was in tears, sharing his struggle with impending bankruptcy and the foreclosure of his home. My heart went out to him, and I couldn't help but wonder how someone who earns so much money could find themselves in such a dire situation. The reality is that many people live beyond their means, falling short month to month because they indulge in excess. Losing your home, resources, income, and belongings can be devastating. I understand this all too well, having experienced such losses myself.

I know what it's like to live on less, and I also know what it's like to have an unlimited income. The period of unlimited income in my life was before the *Soul Dance* era. I owned a beauty empire, and money always flowed to me. Now, post *Soul Dance*, I live in poverty. I rely on the food bank, with a dear friend delivering food to me because I don't drive. I don't own a vehicle, a house, or have any savings to my name. I live day by day, doing the best I can with what I have. This is not a section on how to budget correctly. To tell you the truth, I'm not good at budgeting at all. I totally suck at it, but I get by, and it is necessary, trust me. The truth is, I do budget because it's essential for living a good life. However, when I budget, it doesn't always match what I had planned. Sometimes, I'll get weak and buy a bottle of wine with my grocery money. That's the honest truth of my life. It helps me cope with the emotions I want to bury. But bit by bit, I am learning to process these emotions and explore where they stem from, as we will be discussing in coming chapters.

So let's get into it: I get $1535 Canadian dollars a month. This doesn't get me far, trust me. My room rental is $900, and it is frightening to rent a room when there is a rental shortage across our province. People are ending up homeless because of the housing shortage. When you do find a place to rent, it is sky high in price. I am fortunate enough to have been blessed with decent rental rates. When I first got out of the psychiatric hospital, I rented a room in a rooming house for $450. Then I moved to a place in town for $600. I stayed there for six years and then moved out to the country, where I now pay $900 for a bedroom and an office area to write in. Since moving, I feel rich. I have more space, and it is tranquil and peaceful, thanks to my landlady.

It doesn't come without its downfalls, though. Because I don't drive, I have to take the bus, and it's in the middle of nowhere, surrounded by a forest of trees with bears and cougars. Waiting for the bus causes me great anxiety. I try to get rides into town whenever I can with Susan or her other tenant. I also manage to get my bestie Amy, who lives in my town, to help me with groceries on a weekly or bi-weekly basis if she can. We go on Costco trips together since she has a Costco membership, which I can't afford. I treat Amy to lunch at Costco to thank her for the gas and the membership. It helps me a great deal to bulk up on items like toilet paper and canned goods. Amy also picks me up and we go to the ocean for long walks where we converse about our latest experiences in life.

On this *Soulful Minimalism* journey, I have met a few good friends whom I cherish: like Linda and Gary. They both live in my town and are in the same situation as I am, living with less. Linda, at 76, lives alone in a very modest place and relies on her government pension. Despite her circumstances, she always tells me she feels rich, abundant, and grateful for all that the Great Spirit has given her. Linda and I meet up weekly since we share the same bus route, spending the day together in town. We start with a hearty breakfast at Up Sooke Eatery, chatting about our week, and then run any errands we have before catching the bus back home. It's a simple life, and these outings with Linda are the highlights of my week.

Gary is another friend who I cherish, even though we chat only occasionally. He lives in a rustic cabin by beautiful Kemp Lake. Gary is an artist who spends his time reading, creating art, and playing his guitar. Both Linda and Gary live life with passion on less, and they make it look easy. Their example has been a significant source of inspiration for me, showing me that having friends you can relate to is crucial in life.

Before the COVID outbreak, I used to join local ladies for coffee meetups in town. However, I found these gatherings triggering. I couldn't relate to their way of life—they all had their own homes, money, husbands, and families. I, on the other hand, have no money, no home of my own, no children and an extremely small family. Attending these meetups only made me sad, so I stopped going. The ladies I met at those coffee gatherings were lovely, but I realized that I needed to do some deep inner work to heal the triggers that surfaced during our meetings. These encounters highlighted unresolved feelings within me that I had to address. I discuss my methods for healing these triggers in Chapter Two.

Living on less certainly has its challenges, and the emotions that accompany it are essential to acknowledge and address. It's easy to feel overwhelmed, inadequate, or isolated when you see others living more comfortably. However, it's through understanding and processing these emotions that we find strength and resilience. Embracing a simpler lifestyle can lead to a profound sense of fulfillment and gratitude for what we have, rather than focusing on what we lack. In the following chapters, I will share more about how to navigate these emotional landscapes and find peace and contentment in a life lived with less.

When we're limited with our finances, how do we begin to budget? Well, that can be a challenge, to say the least. But creating a budget is essential. Start by tracking your income and expenses, and make sure your budget outlines your monthly spending. It's crucial to stick to it, as it's very easy to get off track. I find that if I don't keep track of my expenses regularly, it's super easy to lose control of my spending. Personally, I track my expenses the old-fashioned way, in a book. But in today's world, there are plenty of ways to track your spending using apps, spreadsheets, and accounting programs.

One key point that will help you manage your finances better is to cut unnecessary expenses. Reduce or eliminate nonessential items like dining out, subscriptions, impulse purchases, and so on. This was the most difficult part for me. In today's world, everything seems to come with a monthly subscription. When I moved into a higher rental market, going from $600 to $900 for rent, I had to cut down on the subscription services I used. It was hard and emotionally difficult, but I did it. Now I keep just a few subscription services that I can't live without, like my movies and audiobooks, which are my passions.

I know it's important to save money for emergencies, but some people don't understand how difficult this can be when you're living on a tight budget. When you need money to live, it simply doesn't stretch far enough, and saving can seem impossible. However, I have found a way to tap into my passion as an indie author. From my experience, there isn't much money in it—though some people are very successful—but I do it because I'm passionate about helping people and sharing my story. The little money I make from the books I publish goes straight into my savings account. So far, I've saved $130. I smile when I say this because my intent was always to do it for my passion, not for the money. So, all is well in the world.

What I try to do to save money is to purchase high quality items that last longer, instead of buying cheaper ones that wear out quickly. One way to do this is by buying second-hand. Shopping at thrift stores, garage sales, and online marketplaces can yield some great treasures. Linda and I love to go to the local thrift store and see what kind of treasure hunting we can get up to. Sometimes the thrift store has fifty-percent-off days. That is something we always look forward to.

One of the most essential aspects of living on less is cooking at home. Plan your meals to avoid food waste. When I had my beauty empire, it was easy to eat out all the time, and I grew accustomed to this way of living. This habit continued even when I started working part-time to supplement my income, which meant my money didn't stretch as far as I wanted it to. Consequently, I didn't save any money. So, learn from my experience: save your money and cook at home. Plan your meals—you'll thank me later. Food is too expensive to waste so by planning your meals you will most likely have less waste.

Bulk purchases can be handy and save you money, but when you're by yourself, like I am, it can be difficult. So, I stick to non-perishable items to save money, such as canned goods, toilet paper, and laundry detergent. Another tip is to not be afraid to shop for sales, use coupons, and sign up for loyalty programs. If you have the space, growing your own food can be fun and can help with the food bill. I managed to buy myself a small tomato plant and a strawberry plant. It's good for me to care for something other than myself and to have some extra food to eat.

I consider myself lucky that I don't have to pay for utilities such as power, water, and heat. But if you do, and are on a limited income, there are programs that can help make your home as energy efficient as possible. Check with your local government office to see if there are any available programs. When it comes to water, make sure to find and fix any leaks immediately, as they can be very costly. Taking shorter showers can also greatly reduce your water bill.

SOULFUL MINIMALISM

If you drive, consider taking the bus or carpooling. Driving is very expensive nowadays. While it's important and convenient, it's a convenience, not a necessity. I know this is a hard pill to swallow. I used to drive a beautiful sports SUV I named Walter. I drove everywhere. When I had my mental health emergency and lost everything, I lost that vehicle too because I leased it. When the lease was up, so was my money, and I had no choice but to give it up. I transitioned to taking the bus, which was difficult—mostly for my ego—which I lost along the way along with my pride. If taking the bus isn't for you, consider biking or walking. It's a great way to get exercise too.

When it comes to entertainment, it can be challenging. Since I wrote *Soul Dance* and had my mental health emergency breakdown, I not only lost all my physical belongings but also friends and associates. Without a pool of friends to keep me entertained, I got creative. I started to find my passion, which we'll cover in the chapters to come. The new friends I found keep entertained by hiking, kayaking, walking around the ocean, going to the beach, attending community events, visiting the library, and spending time with other friends—all free activities. When I'm not going out with Linda or Amy, I spend my days writing and studying to improve my situation. The more I learn, the better my chances of helping others through my story.

Living on less is not without its challenges, but it can be fulfilling when you focus on what truly matters and make the most of what you have. Remember, before making purchases, ask yourself if they're necessary and if they align with your values and goals. By incorporating these practices into your life, you can reduce your expenses, increase your savings, and find greater satisfaction in living with less.

Reflective Exercises:

1. **Get a Handle on Your Money: Budgeting Your Way**
   Budgeting isn't just about cutting back—it's about getting real with where your money goes and making it work for you. Think of it as a tool to help you prioritize what truly matters in your life.

   - Jot down all your income sources—big or small.
   - Track your spending in categories like rent, groceries, fun stuff, and those sneaky little extras.

- Spot where you can cut back without feeling deprived, and redirect that cash to what you really care about.
- Set some financial goals that excite you, whether it's a vacation fund or saving for a new hobby.
- Notice how taking charge of your finances makes you feel more in control—and maybe even a little less stressed.

Reflection Questions:

- How does setting up a budget change how you see your money?
- Did any of your spending habits surprise you?
- How can you shift spending towards things that make your life better?

1. **Master the Grocery List: Shop Smarter, Not Harder**
   Making a grocery list is more than just planning meals—it's a way to keep things simple and intentional. Plus, it helps you avoid those impulse buys that add up.

- Before you shop, take a quick inventory of what's in your pantry and fridge.
- Plan your meals for the week and write down the ingredients you actually need.
- Stick to your list when you're at the store—see how it feels to shop with purpose.
- Notice how this little habit helps you stay focused and saves you time and money.

Reflection Questions:

- How does using a list change your shopping experience?
- Did you end up spending less or wasting less food?
- How does this practice help you live more intentionally and with less clutter?

1. **Plan Your Meals, Simplify Your Week**

SOULFUL MINIMALISM

Meal planning doesn't have to be complicated. It's all about making your week a little easier by knowing what's on the menu. Plus, it keeps you eating well without the stress.

- Take a few minutes each week to sketch out your meals, including snacks.
- Use a calendar or app if it helps, but don't overthink it—just jot down what sounds good.
- Make a shopping list based on your plan, and see if you can cook in batches to save time.
- Enjoy the feeling of knowing what's for dinner without the last-minute scramble.

Reflection Questions:

- How does planning your meals impact your day-to-day stress?
- Did you notice any changes in your eating habits?
- How does meal planning help you stay in tune with your values of simplicity and mindfulness?

1. **Cut the Digital Clutter: Slim Down Your Subscriptions**
   Subscriptions can sneak up on us, eating away at both our money and attention. It's time to do a quick audit and keep only what you really use and love.

- List out all your subscriptions, from streaming services to apps and magazines.
- Ask yourself if each one brings enough value to stick around.
- Cancel the ones that don't make the cut and enjoy the extra cash and mental space.

Reflection Questions:

- Which subscriptions were easy to drop, and why?
- How much did you end up saving?
- Did you miss any of the services, or did you feel lighter without

them?

1. **Get Creative: DIY and Upcycle Your Way to Less Stuff**
   Embrace your creative side by turning old things into new treasures. DIY and upcycling not only save money but also bring a personal touch to your space.

- Look around your home for items that could use a refresh or repurpose.
- Dive into a DIY project that excites you—whether it's painting an old chair or turning jars into planters.
- Notice the joy that comes from creating something unique with your own hands.

Reflection Questions:

- How does DIY or upcycling make you feel?
- Did you find satisfaction in making or repurposing instead of buying new?
- How does this practice fit into your goals of living sustainably and mindfully?

"Be content with what you have; rejoice in the way things are. When you realize there is nothing lacking, the whole world belongs to you."
—Lao Tzu, 500 BCE.

Chapter Two: The Layers of Healing

In the second step of this formula, we will discuss how to heal and recover. I understand how difficult it can be to get help on this part of the journey; I found it very challenging, but not impossible. I did what I could on my own by seeking out books, guided journals, and online courses to aid me in this journey of discovery. I know that without doing deep inner work, it is difficult to live a passionate life. I have tried, and I found it to be impossible, so I did what it took to get healed on a budget. That is why this topic is the focus of the first chapter.

Your emotions are signposts from your soul, indicating whether you are on the right track in life. The Law of Attraction is the most powerful law in the universe. You are creating your reality every moment of every day with every single thought, either consciously or subconsciously. You cannot take a break from it and decide not to create because creation never stops. Understanding your emotions is crucial. If you fail to understand your emotions, it can turn your life upside down.

Unfelt or suppressed emotions such as anger, resentment, and guilt are dense energies that block your energy and auric fields. If we do not remove these emotional blocks, stored in our auric field energy, we can never truly feel at peace. These blockages can even be passed down from our parents, lingering within us like inherited shadows, influencing our perceptions and responses to life's challenges.

They say recovery is much like peeling an onion, with many layers to uncover. As soon as you release one layer, another one emerges, revealing deeper aspects of yourself that need healing—your traumas and your soul. If you read my memoir, *Soul Dance*, you know that I have had my share of traumas and did my best to recover from them through journaling and writing. During a period of my life, I had a part-time job to supplement my income while on disability, which allowed me to see a counselor for about ten sessions. This helped address surface issues like severe anxiety from working but didn't touch the deep wounds festering inside me. When my job ended, I could no longer afford counseling.

I tried to heal myself through journaling, inner child work, and shadow work. Inner child work involves connecting with your inner child and healing unmet needs, while shadow work dives deep into the darker aspects of ourselves that we hide from public view. I undertook this healing journey alone. After completing *Soul Dance*, I thought my healing was finished, but I quickly realized that wasn't true. I had released a layer, perhaps a few, but many more layers remained.

I was raised in a stable and happy home, attended school, and enjoyed a life full of possibilities. I wore rose-colored glasses until I started writing *Soul Dance*. Only then did I recognize that my seemingly happy home was overshadowed by the traumas my parents endured. Trauma, whether big or small, impacts us deeply. My family's traumas affected me, turning me into an empath. I was also bullied in school. My parents were grieving the loss of my sister Donna, creating a somber household. As a result, I learned not to let anyone worry about me because they already had enough to deal with.

My mother unknowingly lived with bipolar disorder and often got angry at my two eldest sisters. This taught me to avoid bothering her, fearing her anger. Consequently, I kept my bullying experiences to myself, enduring the pain alone. This pattern of not using my voice and not speaking up to defend myself became ingrained in me. Years later, I was sexually assaulted by a man named Paul. This unspoken pain contributed to the development of my own bipolar disorder, which went undiagnosed until my *Soul Dance* days. It was then that I crashed and went on a spiralling spiritual journey. I have since healed from that part of my journey, and the mayhem and chaos that mental illness created.

I now lead a balanced life that is far from chaotic. I have learned that the healing I initially experienced was only a layer or two deep; there was still more to uncover. I realized I had more inner work to do. Small things, like being forced to use my voice, would trigger me. I would refuse to speak up and just handle the situation alone. When I struggled to understand something while studying, I would get angry. This anger stemmed from feeling inadequate, a feeling that dates back to when I was in first grade and couldn't grasp what the teacher was trying to teach me. These triggers made me realize there was more inner work to do. So, I dove deeper into inner child work, shadow work, and self-counseling. I also took life coach training, which helped me understand myself on a deeper, more profound level.

Triggers are reactions to past trauma. They signal that something is not right and needs healing. I am not an expert in trauma or triggers, nor am I a psychologist or registered counselor. However, I have taken counseling courses to help me deal with my own traumas. I'm not here to counsel you, but to help you realize that your emotions are signals from your soul, indicating whether you are on the right track. If you're feeling bad, do a self check-in and ask yourself why you feel this way. I realized that I had been covering up my emotions and had never dealt with them. As I started to heal again after writing *Soul Dance*, I realized that I never processed my emotions. I would cover them up with coping mechanisms like wine. While I can handle my wine, I often used it to hide the emotions that began to surface. When I stopped doing that, I realized I couldn't understand the emotions. I had no idea where they stemmed from until I started to journal and took more courses on healing.

Journaling taught me to heal myself by writing down my thoughts. Much like a mind map, I would draw lines and create a map that led to the emotions I was feeling and why I thought I might be feeling them. I noticed that these emotions always traced back to my early childhood. Emotions such as abandonment and loneliness surfaced because my mother was always busy running the household. Friends would come and go, leaving me feeling lonely and abandoned. Loneliness ran rampant inside me throughout my entire life. Recently, I learned that my sadness after spending time with friends stemmed from these early feelings of abandonment.

Once I started to understand and journal about this emotion, I began to heal as I processed my emotions as they arose. I would start by identifying the emotion or thought: How did this make me feel? Why am I feeling this way? Where does this stem from? From there, I could identify the emotion and let it go. Once I started to process the emotions, label them, and understand their origins, I could understand myself on a deeper level. I noticed that once I processed the emotions, these triggers would not resurface. They would simply pass like a thought.

By understanding my emotions and realizing where they originated from, I became less reactive and more emotionally stable. It was all about understanding them. I soon started to have fewer and fewer reactive emotional moments. Recognizing their origins was key.

Emotional healing takes time. Sometimes it's a short process, other times it's long, but whichever the case, healing will eventually come. Patience and perseverance are invaluable during this journey. The key is to allow the process to unfold naturally as you begin your path of self-discovery. Healing involves understanding where the emotions originated from, and from there, learning to let go. Emotional healing can be so gradual that you may not realize you have healed until someone points it out to you.

What I have realized on my journey is that one of the areas I need to continue healing is learning to trust others enough to open my heart to them. As I mentioned in the introduction, being charged with criminal harassment by my spiritual minister caused me to build a protective wall around myself. This is why I am often quiet in a crowd; I do much better one-on-one. Through soul work, I've realized that my distrust traces back to elementary school when a boy named Jason would run up and punch me so hard in the stomach that I couldn't breathe properly for a long time. These incidents formed deep seated wounds that were never addressed because I kept them to myself. Now, at 56, I am finally dealing with these emotions.

I urge you to take the time to address your emotions, to understand what they might be and where they originated from. If you are unsure what emotions you might be dealing with, here are some to help you identify and understand them.

Positive Emotions

1. Happiness
2. Joy
3. Contentment
4. Excitement
5. Love
6. Gratitude
7. Pride
8. Amusement
9. Awe
10. Relief
11. Hope
12. Empathy
13. Inspiration
14. Peacefulness
15. Confidence

SOULFUL MINIMALISM

Negative Emotions

1. Sadness
2. Anger
3. Fear
4. Anxiety
5. Frustration
6. Disappointment
7. Guilt
8. Shame
9. Loneliness
10. Envy
11. Jealousy
12. Grief
13. Despair
14. Helplessness
15. Hopelessness

Mixed or Complex Emotions

1. Ambivalence
2. Nostalgia
3. Bittersweetness
4. Confusion
5. Embarrassment
6. Regret
7. Suspicion
8. Resentment
9. Curiosity
10. Surprise
11. Boredom
12. Apathy
13. Yearning
14. Anticipation
15. Vulnerability

Emotions Related to Interpersonal Relationships

1. Affection
2. Trust
3. Admiration
4. Sympathy
5. Compassion
6. Gratitude
7. Respect
8. Friendship
9. Love
10. Desire
11. Infatuation
12. Resentment
13. Disgust
14. Contempt
15. Betrayal

Emotions Related to Self-Perception

1. Pride
2. Confidence
3. Self-esteem
4. Self-compassion
5. Insecurity
6. Self-doubt
7. Shame
8. Guilt
9. Worthlessness
10. Empowerment
11. Resilience
12. Fulfillment
13. Ambition
14. Determination
15. Fear of failure

Emotions Related to Situations

1. Hope
2. Despair
3. Stress
4. Calm
5. Relief
6. Anticipation
7. Tension
8. Exasperation
9. Confusion
10. Certainty
11. Dread
12. Excitement
13. Surprise
14. Boredom
15. Restlessness

Healing is essential to your growth and well-being in life. For me, living on a tight budget meant finding ways to deal with these emotional wounds on my own. I turned to short online courses, self-help and psychology books, and guided journals to navigate my healing journey. These resources have been invaluable in helping me understand and process my emotions.

While professional therapy can be incredibly beneficial, it's not always accessible to everyone. That's why it's important to find alternative methods and tools that work for you. In the appendix section of this book, I will provide suggestions for resources that have helped me, including books, and journals with prompts. Remember, healing is a personal journey, and what works for one person may not work for another. Be patient with yourself and open to trying different approaches.

Above all, know that you are not alone in this journey. Many of us are working through our own layers of healing, and by taking the time to address and understand your emotions, you are taking a crucial step towards a more fulfilling and balanced life. Keep going, and trust that with time and effort, you will find the peace and clarity you seek.

Reflective Exercises

1. **Figure Out What Sets You Off**
   Understanding your emotional triggers is the first step in healing. Triggers are those moments, people, or situations that stir up strong emotions, usually connected to past experiences.

- Think back on recent times when you felt a strong reaction, like anger, sadness, or anxiety.
- Jot down what was happening during those moments and who was involved.
- Take note of the context—what was going on that might have contributed to those feelings?

Reflection Questions:

- Do you notice any patterns or themes in what sets you off?
- How do you usually react when you're triggered?
- Are there specific people or situations that seem to push your buttons?
- How do these triggers impact your daily life and relationships?

1. **Look Back at Childhood Wounds**
   Childhood experiences can leave lasting marks. Recognizing those emotional wounds helps you understand their impact on how you feel today.

- Reflect on your childhood and think about the experiences or relationships that hurt or stressed you out.
- Write a letter to your younger self, letting out how you felt during those tough times.
- Consider how these moments have shaped your beliefs, behaviors, and emotional responses now.

Reflection Questions:

- What events or relationships from your childhood still stand out emotionally?
- How did you cope with those experiences when you were younger?
- Are there any recurring themes in the wounds from your past?
- How have these wounds influenced how you see yourself and connect with others?

1. **See How the Past Plays Out Now**
   Old wounds can sneak into your present, showing up in your thoughts, actions, and relationships. Spotting these effects is key to moving forward.

- Think about how your childhood experiences show up in your current life.
- Create a mind map linking your past to your present thoughts and feelings.
- Pinpoint any limiting beliefs or patterns that stem from those old wounds.

Reflection Questions:

- How do your past wounds tie into your current emotional triggers?
- In what ways do these old hurts affect your relationships?
- Do you notice any self-sabotaging habits or negative self-talk connected to your past?
- How do these wounds hold you back from enjoying life?

1. **Make a Healing Game Plan**
   Healing is a journey, not a quick fix. Crafting a personal healing plan can give you a roadmap to follow.

- Think about what actions or practices could help you heal, like therapy, journaling, or meditation.
- Set small, realistic goals for your healing journey.
- Develop a self-care routine that makes you feel good and supports

your emotional well-being.
- Reach out to trusted friends, family, or professionals for support when you need it.

Reflection Questions:

- What healing methods resonate most with you?
- How can you fit these healing practices into your daily routine?
- What little steps can you take regularly to encourage healing and growth?
- How can you create a space that supports your healing process?
- Who can you lean on for support and encouragement?

1. **Be Kind to Yourself**
   Self-compassion is a must when it comes to healing. Treat yourself with the same kindness you'd offer a friend going through a tough time.

- Write down a few affirmations that remind you to be gentle with yourself, and read them often.
- Think about times when you've been hard on yourself, and practice re-framing those thoughts with a kinder perspective.
- Engage in activities that lift you up and make you feel good.

Reflection Questions:

- How do you usually treat yourself when things get tough?
- What can you do to show yourself a little more kindness and understanding?
- How does being kinder to yourself shift your emotional landscape?

"Although the world is full of suffering, it is also full of the overcoming of it."
—Helen Keller

Chapter Three: Power of Forgiveness

I have dedicated an entire chapter to forgiveness because it is essential to the well-being of your soul. I have learned a lot about forgiveness through my spiritual studies, reading, and self-discovery. When I first wrote *Soul Dance*, it was intended as a revenge book—a way to show the people who hurt me what they did. However, by the time I finished writing, it had transformed into a healing book. Soon after, just before writing *Soulful Minimalism*, I forgave them wholly and completely. I even forgave myself for what happened, which was the most challenging part. Before, I did not treat myself well at all and lacked self-love. Now, I take myself into consideration first and foremost.

Through my self-study, I realized I needed to forgive Jason, my childhood bully, and Paul, the rapist. I thought I had forgiven them because I had forgotten about the incidents—or so I thought. I needed to be acknowledged for what happened to me, which is why I wrote about it in *Soul Dance*. By digging deeper into my inner child and shadow self, I discovered that I was not fully healed emotionally because I had not forgiven them or myself.

Forgiveness is a decision to release the resentment, vengeance, or hate you have toward the person or people who harmed you. Remember, it has nothing to do with whether they deserve to be forgiven. It is all about you. Harboring hate, resentment, or vengeance takes energy, and this energy can permeate your cells, potentially causing ailments. That would be a shame.

Forgiveness is about freeing yourself from the heavy burden, anger, and bitterness that take up space in your mind and body. It is an act of kindness you offer to yourself, a crucial part of your healing process—not theirs. By allowing your emotional wounds to heal, you set your soul free.

Forgiveness is about letting go of the pain. If you have truly let go, you have relinquished the power it had over you, and forgiveness becomes the next step in the healing process. You can accept what happened and let go of the hold the incident had on your life.

Some people believe that forgiveness is about excusing or condoning the behavior of those who hurt you. It is not. I used to think that as well. Forgiveness does not condone or excuse harmful behavior; it does not imply that what happened to you was acceptable. It does not mean you need to forget the offense either. You need to acknowledge the hurt but not let it dominate your life. When I first started writing *Soul Dance*, those I needed to forgive dominated my thoughts. I was angry, and that was all I thought of. But now, through the healing process, I have learned to forgive, and it no longer dominates my life.

What I wanted most with *Soul Dance* was reconciliation with those who hurt me, for closure. However, I have begun to realize that might never happen. Forgiveness does not automatically mean reconciliation. When you forgive, it does not mean an automatic relationship with the offender. It is also not a sign of weakness; it requires strength and courage to overcome the negative emotions associated with it.

One of the most challenging tasks for me was forgiving Jason, my childhood bully. I vividly recalled the incident during a meditation session. In my mind's eye, I saw Jason running up to me in the schoolyard and punching me hard in the stomach. The memory was haunting because it symbolized how he had shattered my spirit and soul. Even though I didn't realize it at the time, I was still harboring deep-seated anger towards him.

In meditation, I attempted to forgive Jason repeatedly. Each time, I found myself unable to proceed. This struggle forced me to delve deeper into the impact of his abuse. It became clear that Jason's actions had wounded me more deeply than I had acknowledged. They left me with a lingering sense of self-protection and an underlying distrust of others, which continued to affect me.

To break through this barrier, I shifted my perspective. I imagined Jason's life from his viewpoint—a troubled individual likely struggling with his own pain and upbringing. Viewing him with compassion allowed me to begin forgiving him, a pivotal step in my healing journey.

I forgave Jason not for his sake, but for mine. The benefits of forgiveness far outweighed any reservations I had. After forgiving him, I noticed a profound increase in my inner happiness. I wrote a letter to Jason, detailing the impact of his actions on my life and expressing my forgiveness. Since I had no way of delivering the letter to him, I ceremoniously burned it for closure.

Forgiveness brought great relief, dissipating the anger and resentment that had drained my soul. It cleared away negative emotions and deepened my empathy and understanding of others. Moreover, forgiving Jason alleviated my stress and anxiety levels, significantly improving my overall mental well-being. As someone who battles depression, I found that releasing these negative emotions created mental space for more positive and fulfilling experiences in my life.

Most importantly, forgiving myself alongside forgiving others boosted my self-esteem and sense of self-worth. It taught me the power of self-compassion and resilience, paving the way for a more fulfilling and compassionate journey forward.

The Difference Between Forgiving and Forgetting

Forgiving:

- Forgiveness is a conscious choice to release feelings of resentment or revenge.
- It involves acknowledging the hurt and the offense but choosing to let go of the emotional burden associated with it.
- Forgiving allows you to release negative emotions, leading to emotional and psychological healing.
- It can be a gradual and ongoing process, especially for deep or repeated offenses.

Forgetting:

- Forgetting is often an involuntary, passive process where the memory of an event fades over time.
- It can sometimes involve a form of denial, where one pretends that the offense never happened.
- Forgetting without forgiveness can lead to repeating the same mistakes or allowing the same harmful behavior to occur again.
- Some hurts are too deep to be forgotten, and attempting to forget without forgiving can leave emotional wounds unhealed.

Reflective Exercise: Forgiveness Journal Prompts

1. Identify the Hurt:

- Who or what has caused you pain? Describe the situation in detail.
- How did this experience affect you emotionally, mentally, and physically?

1. Explore Your Emotions:

- How do you feel when you think about this person or event?
- What emotions come up most strongly—anger, sadness, frustration, etc.?

2. Understand the Impact:

- How has holding onto this hurt affected your daily life and relationships?
- In what ways has it held you back from living fully?

3. Consider the Other Person:

- What might have motivated the person to act as they did? Try to see the situation from their perspective.
- Does understanding their perspective change how you feel?

4. Assess Your Readiness to Forgive:

- On a scale of 1-10, how ready do you feel to forgive this person or situation? Why?
- What fears or reservations do you have about forgiving?

5. Define Forgiveness for Yourself:

- What does forgiveness mean to you?
- What would it look like to forgive in this particular situation?

6. Benefits of Forgiving:

- What positive changes might occur in your life if you chose to

forgive?
- How might forgiveness free you or improve your well-being?

1. Release the Hurt:

- Write a letter to the person who hurt you, expressing your feelings honestly. You do not have to send it.
- Imagine letting go of your anger and hurt. Describe how it feels to release these emotions.

2. Self-Forgiveness:

- Is there anything you need to forgive yourself for in this situation?
- How can you show compassion to yourself as you work through this process?

3. Take Action:

- What steps can you take to move towards forgiveness?
- Are there any rituals or practices (e.g., meditation, therapy, talking to someone) that might help you?

4. Reflect on Progress:

- Revisit your previous entries after a few weeks or months. How have your feelings changed?
- What progress have you made towards forgiveness?

5. Gratitude and Growth:

- What have you learned from this experience that you are grateful for?
- How have you grown as a person because of this situation?

Use these prompts as a guide to explore your feelings, process your emotions, and move towards forgiveness. Remember, this is a personal journey, and it's okay to take your time.

KAREN ROSE KOBYLKA

"Forgiveness is not an occasional act; it is a permanent attitude."
—Martin Luther King Jr.

Chapter Four: Journaling Yourself to Recovery

I am a firm believer in journaling. The truth is, I have always journaled. Some would say that I am a journal junkie. I have journals for everything: one for my finances because I love journaling, and it makes me feel better about having to budget; one for my automatic writing; and one for my private thoughts.

My private thoughts journal is a beautiful 8x11 leather-bound journal with the tree of life engraved in the leather on the front. It is spectacular, and I should mention it is pink, my favorite color. I have a book for my meditations that I create with my channeled "collective souls." Basically, I have a journal for most things, even my online courses.

I collect journals so that when I need one, I can go into this box of blank journals and choose the lucky journal that gets to be the next project. My most cherished journal is a leather journal with handmade paper torn around the edges to look antique. This journal was over $40, but it is lovely to look at, with a leather strap to hold it in place. I have yet to use it but have it sitting on the bookshelf as a decoration until a special project comes along. I also have prompt journals that help you start by giving you words, phrases, or questions. I have a bookshelf dedicated to these. This is my passion.

I am passionate about journaling because I know it helps me in so many ways... let's count the ways....

Benefits of Journaling

1. Reduces Anxiety
2. Boosts mood
3. Boosts creativity
4. Boosts confidence
5. Achieve more goals
6. Improves mental health
7. Improves writing skills
8. Clarify thoughts
9. Improves communication
10. Motivates
11. Helps with depression

12. Regulates emotions
13. Greater productivity
14. Greater self-discipline
15. Helps heal trauma

I am sure there are more but that is what I thought of when I think of journalling. Journalling became popular when Julia Cameron came out with her book *The Artists Way*. Julia talks about the morning pages. You write in the morning to dump anything that is mental clutter to free your mind. This way you can be more productive throughout your day.

Overcoming Resistance or Self-Doubt About Journaling

I understand that there are people who can't imagine journalling, they don't write down anything. The fact is you don't have to do it in a book you can do it on the computer, but I feel it doesn't have the same effect.

Starting a journaling practice can sometimes be challenging. Resistance and self-doubt are common obstacles, but they can be overcome with a few mindful strategies. Here are some tips to help you overcome these barriers:

1. Acknowledge Your Feelings: Understand that it's normal to feel hesitant or doubtful about journaling. Acknowledge these feelings without judgment. Recognizing your resistance is the first step toward overcoming it.
2. Start Small: Begin with just a few minutes each day. Set a timer for few minutes and write whatever comes to mind. The key is to start small and gradually increase the time as you become more comfortable.
3. Let Go of Perfection: Remember, your journal is a private space for your thoughts and feelings. It doesn't have to be perfect. Allow yourself to write without worry about grammar or spelling—just be yourself.
4. Use Prompts: If you're unsure what to write about, use journaling prompts to get started. Prompts can provide a focus and make the process less daunting. Start with a prompts to get yourself going on

SOULFUL MINIMALISM

the journaling train such as, "Today, I feel..." or "One thing I'm grateful for is..."

5. Create a Ritual: Establish a journaling routine that feels special. Find a quiet space, light a candle, or play soothing music. Creating a ritual can make journaling a more inviting and enjoyable practice.
6. Write About Your Resistance: Use your journal to explore your resistance. Write about why you feel hesitant or doubtful. Sometimes, simply getting these feelings down on paper can help you understand and overcome them.
7. Focus on the Benefits: Remind yourself of the benefits of journaling. Writing can reduce stress, clarify your thoughts, and enhance self-awareness. Keeping these positive outcomes in mind can motivate you to persist.
8. Practice Self-Compassion: Be kind to yourself throughout the process. It's okay to miss a day or struggle to find the right words. Self-compassion will help you stay committed to your journaling practice.
9. Join a Community: Consider joining a journaling group or community. Knowing others are on the same journey can be incredibly motivating.
10. Reflect on Your Progress: Periodically review your journal entries to see how far you've come. Reflecting on your progress can boost your confidence and reinforce the value of your journaling practice.

By addressing your resistance and self-doubt with these strategies, you can cultivate a rewarding journaling habit that supports your emotional and mental well-being. Remember, the journey of journaling is personal and unique to you. Embrace it with an open heart and mind.

The Benefits of Journaling by Hand

In today's digital age, it might be tempting to keep a journal on your computer or smartphone. While digital journaling has its conveniences, there are distinct benefits to journaling by hand that can deeply enhance your experience:

1. Enhanced Cognitive Processing: Writing by hand engages your brain in a unique way. The act of forming letters and words manually requires different cognitive processes than typing. This can lead to deeper thinking and better memory retention.
2. Mindfulness and Presence: Handwriting forces you to slow down, making the journaling process more deliberate and mindful. This slower pace can help you stay present in the moment, allowing for greater self-reflection and awareness.
3. Emotional Connection: There's something inherently personal and intimate about putting pen to paper. The physical act of writing can help you connect more deeply with your emotions, making your journaling practice a more profound and therapeutic experience.
4. Reduced Digital Distractions: When journaling on a computer or mobile device, it's easy to get distracted by notifications, emails, and other online activities. Journaling by hand removes these distractions, allowing you to focus solely on your thoughts and feelings.
5. Creative Expression: Handwriting allows for more creative expression. You can doodle, draw, and experiment with different handwriting styles. This creative freedom can make your journaling practice more enjoyable and visually stimulating.
6. Physical Connection: Holding a pen and feeling the texture of the paper provides a tactile experience that can be grounding and comforting. This physical connection to your journal can enhance your sense of attachment and dedication to the practice.
7. Better Focus and Clarity: The process of handwriting can help you organize your thoughts more clearly. It encourages you to think more carefully about what you want to say, leading to greater clarity and focus in your writing.
8. Memory and Learning: Studies have shown that writing by hand can improve memory and learning. The action of writing activates different parts of your brain, helping you to better absorb and retain information.
9. Personal Touch: Your handwriting is uniquely yours. A handwritten journal carries a personal touch that a digital document cannot replicate. It becomes a tangible representation of your inner world,

something you can look back on and physically hold in your hands.
10. Timelessness: There's a timeless quality to handwritten journals. They can be cherished keepsakes, passed down through generations, and preserved in a way that digital files may not be. The permanence of pen and paper adds a layer of significance to your journaling practice.

While digital journaling has its place, the benefits of journaling by hand can provide a richer, more meaningful experience. Whether you're jotting down thoughts in a beautiful leather-bound journal or scribbling in a simple notebook, the act of writing by hand can be a powerful tool for self-discovery and healing.

Journaling has been a lifeline for me, especially during the most challenging times. When I struggled with brain health issues, I turned to my journals, spending hours each day pouring out my thoughts and feelings. I was trying to make sense of my inner turmoil, not fully realizing the extent of my mental health challenges. In those moments, journaling saved me. It was my refuge, my confidante, and my guide through the darkness.

The act of writing helped me process emotions and experiences that I couldn't otherwise articulate. My journals were my constant companions, providing a safe space to explore my thoughts and emotions without judgment. Through journaling, I discovered patterns, gained insight, and found clarity in the chaos.

This profound practice led to the creation of my first book, *Soul Dance*. What started as a personal journaling journey evolved into a published memoir, a testament to the transformative power of writing. From there, I developed *Your Soul Dance: a Creative Guided Journal for Memoir Writing*, designed to help others embark on their own journeys of self-discovery and healing. I have also published 16 other journals, and my business biography, *The Beauty Empire*, will be released this winter.

Journaling has always been more than just a hobby for me; it has been a passion and a pathway to greater things. It has guided me through the most difficult periods of my life, helping me to navigate and overcome countless challenges. The simple act of putting pen to paper opened doors to self-awareness, healing, and growth that I never imagined possible.

Through my journals, I have connected with my inner self, discovered my true passions, and found my voice. Journaling has led me to understand myself better, to forgive, to heal, and to embrace my journey with compassion and gratitude. It has been a tool for transformation, allowing me to create a life of purpose and fulfillment.

As you close this chapter and embark on your own journaling journey, I encourage you to embrace the practice with an open heart. Let your journal be a sanctuary for your thoughts, a canvas for your creativity, and a roadmap for your soul's journey. Whether you write for minutes or hours, let the process guide you to deeper self-understanding and healing. Remember, the journey of a thousand miles begins with a single step—or, in this case, a single word. Start writing and see where your journal takes you.

Reflective Exercises:

1. Select a Soulful Journal

Choosing a journal that resonates with you can make the process of journaling more enjoyable and meaningful. The journal should reflect your personality and feel special to you.

- Visit a store or browse online to find a journal that appeals to you aesthetically and emotionally.
- Consider factors such as the cover design, the texture of the paper, and the overall feel of the journal.
- Make it a ritual to set an intention when you first open your journal, dedicating it to your journey of self-discovery and growth.

Reflection Questions:

- What features do you look for in a journal that make it feel special to you?
- How does having a designated journal enhance your journaling experience?
- How do you feel when you open your journal and begin writing?

2. Choose Your Favorite Pen

SOULFUL MINIMALISM

The act of writing can be more enjoyable and expressive when you use a pen that you love. A good pen can make the writing process smoother and more pleasurable.

- Experiment with different types of pens (gel, ballpoint, fountain) to find one that feels comfortable and enjoyable to write with.
- Consider the pen's grip, ink flow, and how it feels in your hand.
- Use this pen exclusively for your journal to create a sense of ritual and continuity.

Reflection Questions:

- How does the choice of pen affect your writing experience?
- What qualities do you appreciate in your favorite pen?
- How does using a special pen contribute to your journaling practice?

3. Daily Reflection: Document Your Day

Writing about your daily activities can help you reflect on your experiences and recognize patterns in your thoughts and behaviors. This practice can also help you build a consistent journaling habit.

- Each evening, take a few minutes to write down what you did during the day. Include details about your activities, interactions, and any notable events.
- Reflect on your feelings and thoughts about the day's events.
- Continue this practice every day for seven days.

Reflection Questions:

- How do you feel about documenting your daily activities?
- What patterns or themes do you notice in your reflections after seven days?
- How has this exercise helped you gain momentum in your journaling habit?

4. Start the Morning Pages

Morning Pages, a concept popularized by Julia Cameron in *The Artist's Way*, involves writing three pages of longhand, stream-of-consciousness thoughts first thing in the morning. This practice helps clear your mind and spark creativity.

- Set aside time each morning to write three pages of whatever comes to mind. Don't worry about grammar, spelling, or structure.
- Use this time to free write, letting your thoughts flow onto the paper without censorship or judgment.

Reflection Questions:

- How does writing Morning Pages affect your mental and emotional state?
- What insights or creative ideas have emerged from this practice?

5. Explore Your Emotions

Journaling can help you process and understand your emotions, providing a safe space to express and explore your feelings.

- Write about your emotions in detail, describing how you feel and why you think you feel that way.
- Reflect on any patterns or triggers you notice in your emotional responses.

Reflection Questions:

- What emotions have you experienced today, and what might have triggered them?
- How do these emotions affect your thoughts and behaviors?
- What strategies can you use to manage your emotions more effectively?

"Write hard and clear about what hurts."
– Ernest Hemingway

Chapter Five: Mindset Mastery

I remember the days before I started to meditate—I felt normal, like a muggle, which is what I call non-magical folk. Although I had heard of meditation, I never really understood its benefits. I had no idea what a mantra was and didn't use affirmations for anything. After my mother died, I turned to the Spiritual Church, which often held classes in the evenings. At one class, I thought I was attending a tarot card class, but it turned out to be an unofficial mediumship circle. A circle is when a group of people gather weekly to practice their mediumship skills. At the beginning of each session, we would meditate. That was my very first-time experiencing meditation. The teacher was phenomenal at leading guided meditations, and from then on, I was intrigued by the practice.

I started with 5-minute meditations and eventually advanced to sessions that lasted an hour. Meditation was healing for me. It filled my heart with joy. After each session, I would journal and receive amazing messages from spirit. I have since gone on to become a meditation teacher, and it is truly one of my passions. I have also developed a journal called *Spiritual Insights*, where you record your spiritual moments after your meditation practice. During meditation, I would get visions, messages, and insights for myself and others in my circle. I felt like I was discovering a new world around me. I also meditate before each intuitive reading to clear my mind and get my energy and vibration ready and at their peak before connecting to the spirit world. I find my connection to spirit is much clearer after I have meditated.

Another tool I use to get into the zone of intuition and channeling my Collective Souls is mantras. The Om mantra is one of the most popular today, and I believe it works because it gets you into an energetic frequency that brings you close to spirit. I also use affirmations, such as "I am loved," "I am enough," and "I am powerful," to get myself into a better mental space. When I find an affirmation that speaks to my soul, I print it out and put it on my bathroom mirror to remind myself to say it daily, keeping me motivated, happy, and vibing high.

Mindset Mastery: Tools for Meditation, Mantras, and Affirmations
Meditation:

Meditation is a practice that involves training the mind to focus and achieve a state of deep relaxation, concentration, and heightened awareness. It has been used for centuries as a tool for spiritual growth, self-improvement, and physical and mental well-being.

There are many different types of meditation, each with its own unique focus and method. Some types of meditation involve focusing on the breath, while others involve the use of a mantra or visualization. Some types of meditation are guided, while others are self-directed.

The goal of meditation is to achieve a state of deep relaxation and mental clarity, in which the mind is free from the constant chatter of thoughts, worries, and distractions. In this state, the mind is able to focus more clearly, be more present in the moment, and access deeper levels of insight and understanding.

Meditation is a simple practice that can be done by anyone, regardless of age, physical ability, or religious beliefs. It can be done in a variety of settings, including in a quiet room, in nature, or even while walking or commuting. It can be done for as little as a few minutes or as long as several hours, depending on the individual's preference and goals.

Meditation Basics

1. Get comfortable sitting upright. Find a comfortable place to sit with your back straight. Sitting upright helps you stay alert and prevents you from falling asleep during meditation. Use a chair, cushion, or bench to support your posture.
2. Relax while staying awake: Allow your body to relax as much as possible while maintaining a state of wakefulness. Release any tension in your muscles but keep your spine straight and your head aligned with your neck and shoulders.
3. Exist in the normal noise around you: Accept the ambient sounds in your environment as part of your meditation practice. Instead of trying to block out noise, let it be. Use it as an anchor to stay present, acknowledging it without judgment.
4. Be present: Focus on the present moment. Let go of any thoughts about the past or future. Ground yourself in the now, fully experiencing each moment as it comes, without distraction.
5. Focus on your breath: Pay close attention to your breath as it flows in

and out of your body. Notice the sensation of the air entering your nostrils, filling your lungs, and then leaving your body. Use your breath as a focal point to anchor your awareness.

6. Take three deep breaths: Start your meditation with three deep breaths. Inhale deeply through your nose, filling your lungs completely. Hold the breath for a moment, then exhale slowly through your mouth. This helps calm your mind and body, preparing you for deeper relaxation.

7. Focus on what you are appreciative of: Spend a few moments reflecting on the things you are grateful for. This practice cultivates a positive mindset and opens your heart, enhancing the quality of your meditation.

8. Place your tongue on the roof of your mouth: Lightly rest your tongue against the roof of your mouth, just behind your front teeth. This position helps reduce tension in your jaw and promotes a sense of calm.

9. Close your eyes: Gently close your eyes to minimize visual distractions. This allows you to turn your attention inward and deepen your focus on your inner experience.

10. Clear your worries and mind chatter: As you settle into meditation, consciously release any worries or mental chatter. Imagine your thoughts as clouds passing by; acknowledge them and then let them drift away.

11. When thoughts enter your mind, let them come and gently release them: It's natural for thoughts to arise during meditation. When they do, simply observe them without attachment or judgment. Acknowledge their presence and then gently let them go, returning your focus to your breath.

12. Let the universe deliver peace and tranquility to you: Open yourself to the peace and tranquility that the universe offers. Visualize a calming light or energy surrounding and filling you, bringing a sense of serenity and balance.

13. Find guidance from The Great Spirit: Seek guidance and wisdom from The Great Spirit, or whatever higher power you believe in. Allow this spiritual connection to provide insight, comfort, and

clarity during your meditation.
14. When finished, write down any thoughts you had during this meditation: After completing your meditation, take a moment to jot down any thoughts, feelings, or insights that came to you. This practice helps you reflect on your experience and track your progress over time.

Benefits of Meditation:

1. Stress Reduction: Meditation helps calm the mind and relax the body, reducing the production of stress hormones like cortisol.
2. Improved Focus and Concentration: Regular meditation practice enhances cognitive function, including attention span and ability to focus on tasks.
3. Emotional Well-being: It promotes emotional stability by fostering a positive outlook and reducing symptoms of anxiety and depression.
4. Enhanced Self-awareness: Meditation cultivates mindfulness, allowing individuals to become more aware of their thoughts, emotions, and behaviors.
5. Better Sleep: By promoting relaxation and reducing stress, meditation can improve sleep quality and duration.
6. Pain Management: It can help reduce perception of chronic pain by altering brain pathways involved in pain processing.
7. Increased Creativity: Meditation stimulates creative thinking and problem solving abilities by quieting the mind and allowing new ideas to surface.

Forms of Meditation:

Although there are many forms of meditation, if you are just starting out, I suggest beginning with guided meditation or trying body scan meditation. These methods help keep your mind focused on specific aspects, making them excellent starting points for beginners.

Guided Meditation:

Guided meditation is a form of meditation that involves following verbal instructions, usually provided by a teacher or a recorded voice. The instructions guide the individual through the meditation process, helping them to focus their attention and achieve a particular state of mind or physical sensation. Guided meditation can include visualization, imagery, and the use of specific phrases or affirmations.

Guided meditation can be helpful for individuals who are new to meditation, as it provides a structure for the practice and can make it easier to focus and achieve a meditative state. It can also be useful for individuals who find it difficult to quiet their thoughts or focus their attention.

Guided meditation can be used to address a variety of physical and mental health conditions, such as stress, anxiety, and insomnia. It can also be used to promote relaxation, improve mood, and increase focus and attention.

Guided meditations can be found in many forms, such as audio recordings, videos, or live sessions led by a teacher. There are many different types of guided meditations available, such as guided imagery and visualization meditations, each with their own specific focus and goals.

It's worth noting that guided meditation is a versatile practice that can be adapted to suit different needs, preferences, and skill levels.

Body Scan Meditation:

Body scan meditation is a mindfulness practice that guides your attention through your body, beginning at your toes and gradually moving up to the top of your head. The practice involves lying down in a comfortable position and focusing attention on different body parts, noticing any sensations, such as tension, warmth or cold, and allowing them to just be, without needing to change them.

The goal of body scan meditation is to increase awareness and understanding of one's physical sensations, to help release tension and stress, and to promote relaxation. The practice can also help individuals to identify areas of the body where they may be holding tension and to develop the ability to release it.

Body scan meditation is often used as a complementary treatment for a variety of physical and mental health conditions, such as insomnia, chronic pain, and anxiety. It can be helpful for people who want to work on developing a deeper understanding of their body and physical sensations, and to promote relaxation and well-being. It can also be integrated with other forms of meditation, such as mindfulness meditation, as it is a form of concentrative meditation that involves focusing the mind on a specific object or phrase.

It's worth noting that body scan meditation is a practice that doesn't require any specific spiritual or religious beliefs to be practiced, it can be done by anyone interested in mindfulness and self-awareness, and it's usually guided by a teacher or a recording.

Mantras:

Mantras are sacred words, phrases, or sounds that are repeated silently or aloud to aid concentration during meditation or to invoke a specific intention. Rooted in ancient spiritual traditions, mantras hold symbolic and vibrational power believed to align the mind and body with higher states of consciousness. They often derive from Sanskrit, the language of ancient Indian scriptures, and their repetition is thought to create a resonance that harmonizes the practitioner's inner being with the universal energies they represent.

Mantras serve various purposes depending on the tradition and personal intention. They can focus the mind, clear mental clutter, and facilitate deep states of meditation by providing a singular point of focus. Beyond meditation, mantras are used to cultivate specific qualities such as compassion, wisdom, or courage. By repeatedly chanting or silently affirming a mantra, practitioners believe they can invoke these qualities within themselves, transforming their inner state and fostering spiritual growth.

Mantras are considered vehicles for spiritual awakening and enlightenment. They are believed to have a transformative effect on consciousness, gradually dissolving egoic tendencies and aligning individuals with their true nature or higher self. In essence, mantras function as potent tools for self-realization and inner exploration, guiding practitioners toward a deeper understanding of their place within the cosmos and fostering a sense of connection to the divine or universal consciousness. Whether used for personal growth, spiritual alignment, or simply to enhance meditation practice, mantras continue to be revered for their profound ability to elevate consciousness and uplift the human spirit.

Benefits of Mantras:

1. Focus and Clarity: Reciting a mantra helps concentrate the mind on a specific intention or goal, improving mental clarity and decision-

making.
2. Stress Relief: Mantras have a calming effect on the nervous system, reducing stress and promoting relaxation.
3. Positive Mindset: They instill positive thoughts and beliefs, reshaping negative thought patterns and promoting optimism.
4. Spiritual Connection: Mantras are often used in spiritual practices to deepen one's connection to a higher power or spiritual beliefs.
5. Empowerment: Regular repetition of mantras reinforces self-belief and self-confidence, empowering individuals to achieve their goals.
6. Cultural Heritage: In cultural contexts, mantras preserve and transmit spiritual and cultural values across generations.

Affirmations:

Affirmations release you from limiting beliefs and allow you to know that the possibilities are unlimited. Affirmations are positive statements that can help you to overcome negative emotions. When you say them often enough you start to believe in them. That is why we often put words and phrases of inspiration on our dream/vision board to help us affirm our utmost wishes and desires.

Benefits of Affirmations:

1. Positive Self-talk: Affirmations help replace negative self-talk with positive, empowering statements about oneself and one's abilities.
2. Goal Achievement: They reinforce goals and intentions, helping individuals stay focused and motivated to achieve them.
3. Increased Self-esteem: Regular use of affirmations boosts self-esteem and self-worth by affirming one's positive qualities and achievements.
4. Stress Reduction: Affirmations counteract stress by promoting a sense of control and optimism in challenging situations.
5. Health Benefits: They contribute to overall well-being by reducing anxiety, improving mood, and supporting mental resilience.
6. Improved Relationships: Positive affirmations can enhance interpersonal relationships by fostering empathy, patience, and understanding.

These practices, when integrated into daily life, can have profound effects on mental, emotional, and spiritual well-being, contributing to a more balanced and fulfilling life.

Reflective Exercises:

1. **Daily Meditation Reflections**
   After each meditation session, take a few moments to jot down your experience. Consider the following prompts:

- What thoughts or emotions came up during your meditation?
- Did you notice any physical sensations or shifts in your feelings?
- How did you feel before starting, and how did you feel afterward?
- Did any insights or messages come to you?

This journaling practice helps you track your journey, gain a deeper understanding of your inner world, and spot patterns over time.

1. **Breath Focus Reflection**
   Spend 5-10 minutes focusing on your breath, then reflect on your experience:

- How did focusing on your breath impact your mindset?
- Did you notice any physical changes or sensations?
- Were you distracted, and how did you handle those distractions?

This exercise sharpens your mindfulness skills and strengthens your ability to stay present.

1. **Mantra Journaling Practice**
   Choose a mantra to repeat during meditation, then reflect on the experience afterward:

- What mantra did you pick, and what drew you to it?
- How did repeating the mantra shape your meditation?
- What thoughts, emotions, or changes did you notice?

SOULFUL MINIMALISM

This helps you explore the impact of specific words or phrases on your mental state.

1. **Daily Affirmation Reflection**
   Choose an affirmation to repeat throughout your day. At the end of the day, take a few minutes to reflect:

- Which affirmation did you use, and why did it resonate with you?
- How did saying the affirmation influence your thoughts and behavior?
- Did you notice any shifts in your mood or mindset?

This helps you see how affirmations can weave into your daily life and the effect they have on you.

1. **Mirror Affirmation Exercise**
   Stand in front of a mirror and repeat your chosen affirmation while looking at yourself. Afterward, journal your thoughts:

- How did it feel to say the affirmation while looking into your own eyes?
- What emotions or thoughts bubbled up?
- Did you notice any shifts in how you see yourself or feel about yourself?

This exercise deepens your self-awareness and self-compassion by directly engaging with your reflection.

1. **Creative Affirmation Expression**
   Use your affirmation as inspiration to create something—a piece of art, a poem, or even a song. Then, reflect on the process:

- How did creating something connect you more deeply to your affirmation?
- What insights or feelings came up while you were creating?
- How did this creative expression affect your relationship with the

affirmation?

This approach allows you to explore affirmations in a fun, expressive way, enhancing your connection to their meaning.

1. **Blended Practice Reflection**
   Combine meditation, mantra, and affirmation into one session. Afterward, reflect on how it felt:

- How did each practice contribute to the overall experience?
- Did you notice any combined effects or new insights?
- How did your mental, emotional, or physical state change from start to finish?

This exercise helps you see how these practices work together to support your spiritual growth.

"Meditation brings wisdom; lack of meditation leaves ignorance. Know what leads you forward and what holds you back and choose the path that leads to wisdom."
– Buddha

Chapter Six: Declutter and Organize

Ever since I can remember, I have been organized and have loved to purge and declutter items from my home. It's as if it's in my blood, a part of who I am. In numerology, which is a practice that assigns mystical significance to numbers based on one's birthdate and name, my life path number is 22. The number 22 is known as the "Master Builder" because it has the ability to turn dreams into reality. It's associated with a higher level of spiritual significance and potential.

People with a life path number of master number 22 have a clear vision for the future and the skills to inspire others to work towards that vision. They can see the bigger picture and are driven to create systems and structures that benefit society. One of my passions with being a number 22 is decluttering, organizing and decorating.

Decluttering and organizing are not just about tidying up physical spaces; they are about creating an environment that supports your mental and emotional well-being. A well-organized space can significantly reduce stress, increase productivity, and promote a sense of calm and control. For me, the process of decluttering is almost therapeutic. It allows me to release what no longer serves me and make room for what truly matters.

In this chapter, I will share the methods and strategies that have worked for me in my journey to maintain an organized life. We'll explore practical tips for decluttering, how to create and maintain organizational systems, and the benefits of living in a space that reflects order and simplicity. Whether you're naturally inclined towards organization like I am, or if it's something you find challenging, I hope to provide you with insights and inspiration to help you create a harmonious living environment.

Although I don't claim expertise in Feng Shui, I recognize its effectiveness. Feng Shui is an ancient Chinese practice that harmonizes people with their surrounding environment by focusing on the flow of energy, known as "Chi". What resonates with me about Feng Shui is its emphasis on energy. If you appreciate energy as much as I do, you'll understand that reducing clutter and enhancing organization can significantly impact well-being and balance.

From what I've gathered about Feng Shui, creating clean and uncluttered spaces allows positive energy to flow freely. Clear hallways and doorways facilitate smooth energy flow, while organized countertops contribute to a sense of order. For me, these principles hold true. They aren't just guidelines; they're pathways to cultivating a space that invites positive energy and promotes overall well-being. By embracing these principles, you can create an environment that not only looks orderly but also supports a harmonious flow of energy throughout your home.

I understand the financial challenges of living on a tight budget. Purchasing new items can feel daunting when resources are limited. I've been on the poverty train, and I know the fear that creeps in when considering decluttering: "What if I need this later and can't afford to replace it?"

But here's a truth I've learned firsthand: living out of a suitcase for even just 30 days can reveal the difference between what we truly need and what we simply accumulate. I did this for a year during my *Soul Dance* days, and it taught me a valuable lesson about the excess stuff that clutters our lives and creates chaos in our energetic space. During this time, I wanted nothing more than what I had. There was never a feeling of wanting more or needing more. I was content.

Times were tough for me during this period, but living out of a suitcase was the easy part. I had just enough of every item: pants, shorts, undergarments, tops, and toiletries. I also had a single photo album that I eventually got rid of by scanning the pictures onto a memory stick, making it much easier to carry around. Additionally, I had a journal and a pen. That was it. Everything else I discarded, and I lived a minimalist lifestyle for a little over a year.

This experience taught me the true value of simplicity. With just a few essential items, I felt liberated and free from the weight of unnecessary possessions. My suitcase held only what I genuinely needed, and that brought me a profound sense of peace and clarity. It made me realize how much excess stuff we accumulate, often without even realizing it, and how it can clutter not just our physical space but our minds as well.

Living with less helped me focus on what truly mattered. I wasn't distracted by material possessions or the constant desire for more. Instead, I could fully engage with my experiences and the people around me. This minimalist approach created a sense of harmony in my life, allowing me to live more intentionally and mindfully.

Decluttering and organizing are not just about tidying up your physical space; they are about creating a more meaningful and purposeful life. By letting go of what you don't need, you make room for what truly enriches your life. This process can be incredibly empowering, helping you to break free from the consumerist mindset and embrace a lifestyle that aligns with your values and goals.

So, as you embark on your journey towards minimalism, remember that it's not about depriving yourself but about discovering the freedom and contentment that come with living with less. By decluttering your space and organizing your belongings, you can create an environment that supports your well-being and allows you to focus on what truly matters.

The readiness to let go is essential. Being an organizing expert doesn't mean I don't empathize with the reluctance to purge, especially when possessions are scarce. For example, I once accumulated multiple sets of pajamas—gifts from my sister, purchases, and seasonal variations—filling up two drawers. To some, this might seem harmless, but in limited space, it became clear it wasn't necessary.

Recently, during a move, I faced the task of sorting through my meticulously organized room. What I discovered was unnecessary clutter—clothes and books I had no use for and no interest in. I had to ask myself: "Will I ever use this? Do I truly need it?" The answer was often no. I realized I only need a few favorite pairs of pajamas—one for each season—neatly fitting into a single drawer. This simplicity ensures I always have what I need without clutter or chaos.

This principle applies to everything else too. Ask yourself: Does it serve a purpose? Does it fit well into my life? Is it something I truly enjoy? Answering these questions honestly while sorting through your belongings helps distinguish clutter from what truly adds value to your life.

What I've noticed is that people tend to accumulate too many of certain items. Take towels, for instance. You only need two towels per person in the house: one for use and one as a backup. However, many people have multiple towels, which take up space and add to the clutter in their lives. I suggest minimizing the number of items you actually have, just like I did with my pajamas. By reducing excess, you can create a more organized and streamlined living environment.

One strategy that has worked wonders for me is the "one in, one out" rule. For every new item that comes into my home, an old item must go. This keeps my space from becoming overcrowded and ensures that everything I own is something I genuinely need or love.

Ultimately, I've come to understand that having a few quality items I love and use regularly is far more fulfilling than having excess. When you surround yourself with things that bring joy and comfort, they positively influence your energy field and contribute to a sense of well-being. This is not just about having a tidy home, but about creating an environment that supports and nurtures you.

Decluttering and organizing aren't just tasks; they are transformational practices that can enhance your life. As you let go of the unnecessary, you make room for new opportunities, positive energy, and a deeper connection with yourself. So, take the plunge, start small, and watch as your space—and your life—transforms for the better.

Decluttering can reduce stress and anxiety, increase productivity and focus. If I don't have you convinced yet there are more benefits; decluttering creates a more inviting and comfortable living environment. It also enhances overall sense of control and satisfaction.

Clutter varies across different areas of life—physical, digital, and emotional—and can differ from person to person. Generally, clutter refers to anything that is messy, unorganized, excessive, or overwhelms a space. It can manifest as physical objects crowding a room, digital files filling up a hard drive, or emotional baggage weighing on the mind.

There are many causes of clutter such as mental health issues, emotional attachments, lack of organizational systems, and accumulation over time.

The Decluttering Process

Create a Plan

- Breaking Down the Process: Divide the decluttering process into manageable steps to avoid feeling overwhelmed.
- Prioritize One Area: Focus on one specific area to tackle first, such as a closet or a drawer, to make the task feel more achievable.

Gathering Supplies

- Note-taking: Have a pad and paper ready to make notes and lists.
- Tools: Gather boxes, bins, labels, and other necessary tools to help sort and organize items.

Establishing a Timeframe

- Schedule Sessions: Dedicate specific times for decluttering sessions to ensure consistency.
- Maintain Momentum: Keep the momentum going by sticking to your schedule and celebrating small wins.

Starting Small

- Begin with a Small Area: Start with a small, manageable area to build confidence.
- Build Motivation: Success in small areas will motivate you to tackle larger spaces.

Sorting and Categorizing

- The Four-Box Method: Use four boxes labeled Keep, Donate, Sell, and Trash to sort items.
- Create Meaningful Categories: Develop categories that make sense for your lifestyle to simplify the sorting process.

Dealing with Different Types of Clutter

- Paperwork and Mail: Sort through paperwork and mail, keeping only what's necessary.
- Clothing and Accessories: Review your wardrobe, keeping items you wear regularly.
- Kitchen and Pantry Items: Discard expired items and organize the rest for easy access.
- Books and Media: Decide which books and media to keep, donate,

or digitize.
- Sentimental Items: Carefully review sentimental items and decide which ones hold true value.

Let Go of the Old

- Donate or Discard: Get rid of items that are broken, unused, or hold negative memories.
- Keep What You Love: Retain only the items that you love and use regularly.

Organize with Intention

- Storage Solutions: Use baskets, bins, and other storage solutions to keep things organized and out of sight.
- Label Containers: Clearly label containers to make it easy to find and put away items.

Daily Habits

- Daily Tidying: Spend a few minutes each day tidying up and putting things back in their designated places.

Regular Purging

- Review Belongings: Periodically review your belongings and let go of items that no longer serve you.

Establishing Routines and Systems

- Maintenance Habits: Develop daily, weekly, and monthly habits to maintain order.
- Prevent Future Clutter: Implement systems to prevent clutter from accumulating again.

Digital Decluttering

- Organize Digital Files: Keep your digital files and emails organized.
- Reduce Digital Distractions: Unsubscribe from unnecessary emails and organize your digital space.

Developing New Habits

- Mindful Consumption: Practice intentional living by being mindful of what you bring into your home.
- Regular Review: Continuously reassess your belongings and habits to stay clutter-free.

Adopting a Minimalist Mindset

- Quality over Quantity: Embrace the philosophy of owning fewer, but higher quality items.
- Joy of Less: Understand and appreciate the joy and freedom that comes with owning less.
- Organize Photos: Scan and digitize photos to reduce physical clutter.
- Use Audiobooks: Consider using audiobooks instead of physical books to save space.

So now that we've covered the basics of the decluttering process, remember that this chapter is just the beginning. Decluttering and organizing are more than just tidying up; they're about creating space for what truly matters in your life. Remember the mantra: if you don't use it, lose it. Don't hold onto things out of habit or obligation. Instead, be willing to seek out quality over quantity. Clearing your space and organizing your life takes courage and commitment, but the rewards are immense. You'll find clarity, peace, and a renewed sense of energy flowing through your environment. I'm passionate about this topic because I believe in the power of energy and its impact on our well-being.

I firmly believe that energy permeates everything around us. When you begin to rearrange, organize, and declutter your surroundings, you align yourself with the natural flow of the universe. This process not only clears physical space but also creates room for spiritual and emotional growth. As you purify your environment, you'll notice synchronicities and opportunities unfolding in mysterious ways, guiding you closer to what truly resonates with your soul's journey in life. Trust in this process, for it is a powerful catalyst for transformation and alignment with your deepest desires.

Reflective Exercise:

1. The One Suitcase Experiment

Reflecting on a moment when I was faced with homelessness, I recall giving away all my possessions and departing with just one suitcase. This experience left an indelible mark on my soul because it revealed what truly mattered to me. In that moment, I realized I had everything essential and nothing more – just me, my pillows, and that solitary suitcase.

This pivotal experience transformed my perspective and led me to adopt a minimalistic lifestyle. I discovered that material possessions no longer held the same significance. Despite having lived a luxurious life previously, unforeseen circumstances, chronicled in *Soul Dance*, forced me into a minimalist lifestyle. Little did I know, my soul journey had just commenced.

I now understand that true happiness doesn't come from things; it comes from people, nature, and life itself, if you choose to perceive it that way. In this exercise, you'll conduct an inventory of your possessions and then consider what you could bring with you if limited to just one suitcase.

Everything possesses energy, and excess clutter can hinder our thoughts, feelings, and actions. Through this experiment, explore the transformative power of simplicity and recognize the profound impact it can have on your journey of self-discovery.

If you are brave enough to seriously live as a minimalist and declutter your life, this exercise will have you embracing minimalism in no time.

Objective:

To explore the concept of minimalism and assess the significance of material possessions in your life. Through the One Suitcase Experiment, gain insights into what truly matters to you on a deeper level and identify the essence of your priorities.

Step 1: Prepare Your Suitcase

- Get your largest suitcase.
- Pick out your bare essentials that you will need for one month, just as if you are going away on a long vacation to a cabin somewhere. Think

about clothing, toiletries, essential gadgets, and a few personal items that bring you joy.
- Make a detailed list of what you have packed in the suitcase when you first start. This will help you keep track of your essentials and evaluate them later.

- Recall a time in your life when you had to make choices about what to keep and what to leave behind.
- Identify and list possessions that hold the most value to you.

- Provide a brief explanation for each item's significance.

- Consider the emotional attachments associated with each item.
- Evaluate how these emotional connections contribute to your overall well-being.

- Assess the impact of material possessions on your happiness and fulfillment.
- Reflect on whether possessions contribute significantly to your well-being.

Step 2: Live Out of the Suitcase

- For the next 30 days, live solely out of this suitcase. Resist the temptation to grab anything outside of it unless absolutely necessary.
- As you go through each day, pay attention to how you feel about living with just these items. Do you miss anything? Do you find that some items are not as essential as you thought?

Step 3: Reflect and Journal

At the end of each week, reflect on your experience. Ask yourself:

- How did it feel to live with only the items in your suitcase?
- Were there any items you didn't use at all? If so, why?
- Was there anything you found yourself missing or wishing you had

packed?
- Did this experiment change your perspective on what you truly need?

Step 4: Evaluate and Adjust

After 30 days, review the list you made at the beginning. Compare it with your reflections.

- Remove items that you didn't use or that didn't add significant value to your life.
- Consider why you might have thought these items were essential initially and what changed.

Step 5: Take Action

Use the insights gained from this experiment to declutter and organize your living space.

- Let go of items that no longer serve a purpose or bring you joy.
- Simplify your environment based on what you learned about your true needs.

Bonus Tip: Maintain the Minimalist Mindset

- Even after the experiment, continue to question the necessity of new items before bringing them into your home.
- Regularly reassess your belongings to ensure they align with your minimalist values and lifestyle.

By engaging in the Suitcase Experiment, you will not only declutter your physical space but also gain a deeper understanding of what truly matters to you. This exercise is a powerful step toward living passionately with less.

2. Pick One Room in Your Home and Declutter and Organize It

- Choose a room that you use frequently, such as your bedroom, kitchen, or living room. Start by removing all items from the room and sorting them into categories: keep, donate, recycle, or discard. Take your time to thoughtfully decide where each item belongs and re-organize the room to be functional and clutter-free. Reflect on how the newly organized space feels and the impact it has on your daily life.

3. Think About Why You Keep Certain Items. Write Down How They Make You Feel. Do These Feelings Help You?

- As you go through your belongings, pause to consider the emotional attachment you have to each item. Write down the memories and feelings associated with these items. Ask yourself if these feelings are positive or negative. Determine if holding onto the item is beneficial for your well-being or if it's time to let it go. Reflect on how releasing items that no longer serve you creates space for new experiences and growth.

4. List Areas or Items to Declutter. Rank Them by Importance. Reflect on Why You Chose This Order.

- Create a comprehensive list of all the areas and items you want to declutter in your home. Rank them from highest to lowest priority based on factors such as the frequency of use, the level of disorganization, and the emotional weight they carry. Reflect on why certain areas or items are more critical to address first. Consider how tackling high priority items can lead to a more significant impact on your living environment and mental clarity.

5. List Your Possessions as 'Needs' and 'Wants.' Reflect on Why Each Item Is Necessary or Is Just a Desire.

- Divide your belongings into two categories: needs (essential items for daily living) and wants (non-essential items that bring joy or comfort). Reflect on why each item is categorized as a need or want. Consider the functionality, frequency of use, and emotional significance of each item. This exercise can help you prioritize what to keep and what to let go of, fostering a more minimalist and intentional lifestyle.

6. Make a Step-by-Step Decluttering Plan. Reflect on the Time and Tools You Need. How Will You Stay Motivated?

- Outline a clear, step-by-step plan for your decluttering process, including specific tasks, deadlines, and necessary tools (e.g., storage bins, labels, trash bags). Reflect on the realistic amount of time each task will take and schedule it into your calendar. Think about strategies to stay motivated, such as setting small, achievable goals, rewarding yourself after completing tasks, or enlisting the help of a friend or family member for support.

7. After Decluttering, Note How the Change Affects Your Mood and Productivity. Write About These Differences.

- Once you have decluttered and organized a space, take time to observe any changes in your mood, energy levels, and productivity. Write about how the decluttered environment makes you feel—whether it's more peaceful, energized, or focused. Reflect on specific ways the organized space has improved your daily routines, efficiency, and overall well-being.

8. Think About What Leads to Clutter in Your Life. Write Down Strategies to Prevent It.

- Consider the habits and behaviors that contribute to clutter in your home, such as impulsive shopping, not having designated storage spaces, or procrastination. Write down specific strategies to prevent clutter from accumulating in the future. These strategies might include setting regular decluttering sessions, creating a one-in-one-out rule for new items, or establishing a daily tidying routine. Reflect on how these proactive measures can help maintain a clutter-free and harmonious living environment.

9. Pay Attention to Your Thoughts and Feelings While Decluttering. Write About How This Helps You Make Better Choices.

- As you go through the decluttering process, be mindful of your thoughts and emotions. Notice any resistance, attachment, or relief you feel when deciding the fate of each item. Write about how this awareness helps you make more intentional and thoughtful choices about what to keep and what to let go of. Reflect on the personal insights you gain from this process and how it contributes to your overall growth and clarity.

10. Reflect on Your Decluttering Journey. Celebrate Small Wins and Write About How They Make You Feel.

- At the end of your decluttering journey, take time to reflect on the entire process. Celebrate small victories, such as completing a room or organizing a specific category of items. Write about how these accomplishments make you feel and the positive changes you've experienced. Reflect on the lessons learned and the sense of empowerment and liberation that comes from creating a more organized and intentional living space.

> *"The greatest wealth is to live content with little."*
> – Plato

Chapter Seven: Choosing Supportive Relationships

I believe that energetically, people gravitate toward us if we are vibrationally aligned with them. Source energy, or what some call God, will not put anyone in our path who does not resonate with our energy. This understanding comes from the teachings of Abraham-Hicks, and for me, it holds true.

Have you ever noticed that as you grow, some people drift away from your life? Has this ever happened to you? I know it has happened to me. For instance, one of my oldest friends stopped talking to me when I started to work again after my brain health issues. She had her own struggles, and when I expressed gratitude for my hairstyling career, she reacted angrily, saying, "Unlike me, who has no career?" I tried to mend the conversation, but soon after, she stopped calling me. I grieved the loss of this friendship because she was like a sister to me.

As I reflected, I realized that we were no longer vibrationally aligned. While I continued to grow and expand, she did not, and our energies no longer matched. It was a sad realization, but it also highlighted an important truth: this friend was never truly supportive of me.

What I know for sure is that we need to be more selective when it comes to our relationships. Everyone is different, and we all react differently to situations. This chapter is about finding and nurturing supportive relationships that bring joy into our lives. It is about surrounding ourselves with people who uplift us and help us grow.

Supportive relationships are crucial for our well-being and personal growth. They provide a safe space for us to express ourselves, share our dreams, and face our challenges. Supportive friends and family members encourage us, believe in us, and help us stay motivated. They celebrate our successes and comfort us in times of need.

As humans, we thrive when we are with our tribe. The trick is to select a tribe that will feed your soul and be good for your emotional well-being. Anything less than that does not serve you and needs to be healed or let go. It's as simple as that. I understand this is not an easy task, but it's something that should be done sooner rather than later because your emotional well-being is the most important thing in the world. It is what fuels you and helps you thrive in life. Emotional well-being is what leads you to a passionate life.

When my brain health first began to decline, I was thriving within my spiritual tribe. I write about this in *Soul Dance*. I was on fire, feeling supported and loved within this community. Then, I became ill. I lost my tribe of spiritually minded people, as well as my business associates and others who surrounded me. When I regained my health, I had to rebuild my tribe from scratch.

Now, I have a very small circle of friends whom I cherish dearly. A few of them knew me before my brain health issues; the rest knew me after. I share this part of my journey because I understand how difficult it is to lose people and to let them go. It can be very challenging.

I remember when I was married. I lived with a man named Samuel for 13 years. Our relationship was like trying to fit a square peg in a round hole—difficult, emotionally draining, and full of ups and downs. More downs than ups. I lived like that for over 13 years. To cope with the situation, I engrossed myself in work. I grew my beauty empire and became a workaholic, using work as a coping mechanism to help me forget how unhappy I really was. I thought that was my life sentence—to live with Samuel in a mediocre life. So, I became depressed and felt something was missing deep inside my soul. I felt empty.

Then one day, the universe decided I needed a change. I write about this in my book *Soul Dance*. The bottom line was I knew I needed to make a move, so I split up with my common-law husband, Samuel. It was one of the hardest things I have ever done. I thought that he was my forever. He was also my financial security for the future. We had a nice home together, and I left it all behind, taking nothing but a carload of stuff.

Leaving relationships that no longer serve you can be difficult. I understand this because it was that for me. Samuel did not want to go to counseling, so there was no fixing the situation. Sometimes you can heal it with counseling, but sometimes you need to just let it go. That is a positive turn in the right direction. I understand that it is difficult. I still think about Samuel and the choices that I made. Sometimes when I was depressed, I would think to myself, "Did I make the right choice?" I also had dreams about Samuel and how safe he was for me, feeling in the dream that I was heading home to him because it felt safe.

These dreams and feelings disappeared after a long while. But I can tell you from my experience, I am much happier as a result of leaving. I live my life on my terms. Don't get me wrong, relationships are all about compromise—the give and take. But remember, only stay if you can heal it and are truly happy on a soul level. Anything else is not good enough. Remember, you are worthy of passionate living.

It might not always be easy to determine if a relationship is toxic or not. I suggest using your gut instinct—everyone has one. Notice how you feel when you're in the relationship. Start by writing down your emotions every day; soon, you'll become aware of which relationships serve you and which ones do not.

When the journey of *Soul Dance* began with my brain health issues, I became manic and went into psychosis. During this time, I changed my cell phone number and told no one. This little experiment taught me who was truly there for me during difficult times and who was not. It revealed the value of true friendship and positive relationships. The people who truly cared were the ones that came looking for me. It was an interesting experiment to say the least.

Healthy relationships greatly enhance our overall well-being. When we surround ourselves with supportive, encouraging, and loving people, we experience a sense of upliftment and energy that propels us forward. These relationships act as a source of strength, providing emotional support during tough times and sharing in our joy during moments of success. They help us see the best in ourselves and motivate us to pursue our passions and dreams.

Positive relationships can be compared to a garden—when tended with care and attention, they flourish and bloom. They offer us a safe space to express our true selves without fear of judgment, and in turn, we provide the same for others. This mutual respect and admiration create a cycle of positivity that nurtures our soul and energizes our spirit.

In every relationship, there is an energetic exchange that occurs between individuals. This exchange can be thought of as an invisible flow of energy that passes back and forth, influencing how we feel and behave. When we interact with others, we give and receive energy in various forms, such as emotions, thoughts, and actions. This dynamic plays a crucial role in determining the quality and impact of our relationships.

SOULFUL MINIMALISM

In positive relationships, the energetic exchange is balanced and healthy. Both parties give and receive energy in a way that is uplifting and nourishing. This can manifest through acts of kindness, words of encouragement, shared laughter, and genuine empathy. Such interactions leave us feeling rejuvenated and inspired, ready to tackle the challenges of life with a renewed sense of purpose.

Toxic relationships can sap our energy and leave us feeling exhausted. These relationships often involve one-sided exchanges where one person takes more than they give, leading to an imbalance that can be emotionally exhausting. Over time, this drain can affect our mental and physical health, making it essential to recognize and address such dynamics.

Understanding the concept of energetic exchange allows us to be more mindful of the relationships we cultivate. It encourages us to seek out connections that are mutually beneficial and to let go of those that do not serve our highest good. By being aware of how we exchange energy with others, we can create and maintain relationships that uplift and energize us, contributing to our overall sense of happiness and fulfillment.

We can become accustomed to putting up with negative relationships, but how can we determine which relationships are supportive and which ones are not? It sounds easy, but let's define the characteristics of a positive, supportive person: they are encouraging and uplifting, honest but kind, respectful of boundaries, and they share similar values and goals as you. In contrast, a negative, unsupportive person is constantly critical or judgmental, draining and demanding, disrespectful of boundaries, and engages in gossip or negativity.

So, how do we go about distancing ourselves from negative people? The trick is to gradually reduce contact and be honest but firm about your needs. Focus on setting and maintaining boundaries. It's not easy, but it is worth it for your personal peace in the end. Getting involved in positive groups and meetups is one way to meet like-minded, positive people. Be open to new connections. I know it can be difficult to meet new people, especially if you've closed yourself off in the past, as I wrote about in *Soul Dance*. But working on being more open can lead to meeting more positive people and enriching your life.

Remember, choosing supportive relationships is an ongoing process. It's about aligning yourself with people who uplift and energize you, and letting go of those who drain and diminish your spirit. As you continue on this journey of self-discovery and growth, trust in your ability to attract the right people into your life. Surround yourself with positivity, set healthy boundaries, and watch how your life transforms. You deserve to live a life filled with joy, passion, and supportive relationships that nurture your soul.

To cultivate supportive relationships, we need to be intentional about the people we allow into our lives. Here are some key points to consider:

1. Seek Positive Energy:

Surround yourself with people who radiate positivity. These individuals will inspire and motivate you. Their energy will uplift you and help you maintain a positive outlook on life.

1. Look for Mutual Support:

Ensure that your relationships are balanced, where both parties give and receive support.

1. Communicate Openly:

Share your thoughts, feelings, and concerns with your loved ones. Encourage them to do the same.

1. Set Boundaries:

Healthy boundaries are essential for maintaining supportive relationships. Be clear about your needs and limits. Respect the boundaries of others as well.

1. Let Go of Toxic Relationships:

Identify relationships that drain your energy or bring negativity into your life. It may be difficult, but letting go of toxic relationships is necessary for your well-being.

SOULFUL MINIMALISM

1. Practice Self-Compassion:

Be kind to yourself and recognize that you deserve supportive and loving relationships. Show yourself the same kindness and understanding that you give to others.

By following these principles, you can create a network of supportive relationships that will enhance your journey towards passionate living. Remember, the people you surround yourself with can have a profound impact on your happiness and personal growth. Choose wisely and nurture the relationships that bring joy and positivity into your life.

Reflective Exercise:

Ask yourself the following questions and journal about them to gain deeper insight into your relationships and how they impact your life:

1. Is the relationship serving your highest good?

Reflect on whether this relationship aligns with your values and aspirations. Does it uplift you, inspire you, and help you become the best version of yourself? Write about specific instances where the relationship has positively influenced your growth and well-being.

1. Is the relationship negatively impacting your life in any way?

Consider if this relationship brings stress, anxiety, or negativity into your life. Identify any patterns or behaviors that are harmful or draining. Write about how these negative impacts manifest and how they affect your mental, emotional, and physical health.

1. What can I do to heal the situation?

Think about proactive steps you can take to improve or resolve issues within the relationship. This might include open communication, setting boundaries, seeking mediation, or making personal changes. Journal about specific actions you can take and the potential outcomes you hope to achieve.

1. How do I feel after spending time with this person?

Pay attention to your emotional state after interactions with this person. Do you feel energized, happy, and fulfilled, or do you feel drained, upset, and unvalued? Write about your feelings and consider what these emotions reveal about the nature of the relationship.

1. Do they support my goals and dreams?

Reflect on whether this person encourages and supports your ambitions and aspirations. Are they genuinely interested in your success and happiness, or do they undermine or dismiss your goals? Write about specific instances where they have shown support or lack thereof.

1. Are they respectful and kind?

Consider how this person treats you and others. Are they respectful, considerate, and kind in their words and actions? Do they hear you out and respect your opinions? Write about moments where their behavior demonstrated respect and kindness, or where it fell short.

7. If you had only 5 minutes to live, who would you spend that time with and why?

Reflect deeply on this question. Think about the person or people who matter most to you and why they hold such significance in your life. Consider their impact on your happiness, well-being, and sense of connection. Write in your journal about who you would choose to spend those precious final moments with and the reasons behind your choice. This exercise can help you identify the most meaningful relationships in your life and understand the value they bring.

8. Journal about the cell phone experiment:

SOULFUL MINIMALISM

Imagine not using your cell phone for an entire week. Reflect on who you think would reach out to you during this time and why. Consider who would notice your absence and make an effort to check in on you. Write in your journal about your thoughts and feelings regarding who would come calling and what this reveals about your relationships. This is a hypothetical exercise for personal introspection only; you do not need to actually carry out the experiment. Ponder on the quality and depth of your connections and how you can nurture and strengthen the supportive relationships in your life.

By journaling about these questions, you can gain clarity on the quality of your relationships and make informed decisions about nurturing those that support your highest good while addressing or letting go of those that do not. This reflective process will help you cultivate a supportive and empowering social circle that aligns with your journey toward passionate living.

"I always deserve the best treatment[1] because I never put up with any other."
—Jane Austen

---

1. https://www.ellevatenetwork.com/articles/7666-3-simple-ways-to-develop-empathy-for-your-users

Chapter Eight: Finding Your Passion: Your Life's Purpose

I have always been a passionate person, pouring my soul into projects when I felt aligned with them both energetically and emotionally. When I liked what I did, I was passionately on fire with it. This began at a young age; I was always passionate about art and the urge to create something. As I got older, my career became my passion, a driving force that fueled my ambitions. However, when my career disappeared due to my brain health issues, I found a new passion in spirituality. This spiritual journey fed my soul and became a vital part of my life, aligning perfectly with what I believe is my soul's blueprint.

I believe that each human has a soul's blueprint, a universe led design that outlines the wonderful life we are meant to live and experience. This blueprint also includes our purpose in life. Over the years, I have taken courses on the soul's blueprint and have found it to be a truly fascinating concept. This idea is derived from many different traditions and spiritual teachings, all converging on the belief that our lives have a deeper meaning and purpose.

Understanding that we are destined to be something greater than we realize is both humbling and empowering. It suggests that each of us has a unique path to follow, filled with opportunities for growth, fulfillment, and contribution. This is what I believe constitutes our life's purpose.

Our life's purpose is not just about achieving grand goals or attaining success in the conventional sense. It's about discovering what makes us come alive, what fills our hearts with joy, and what drives us to get up each morning with a sense of excitement and anticipation. It's about aligning our daily actions with our deepest values and passions, and in doing so, contributing to the world in a meaningful way.

The journey to uncovering our life's purpose can be complex. It often involves exploring our interests, talents, and the things that bring us joy. It requires us to listen to our inner voice, to pay attention to the subtle nudges from the universe, and to be open to the signs and synchronicities that guide us along our path.

By understanding and embracing our life's purpose, we can live with greater intention, passion, and joy. We can navigate the challenges and uncertainties of life with a sense of direction and clarity, knowing that each step we take is part of a larger, divine plan.

I always thought my life purpose was to be a hairstylist and makeup artist for the stars. I achieved that goal, yet it didn't feed my soul. It wasn't until my mother passed away that I discovered my passion for mediumship and spirituality. As a born medium, I have always been able to see and sense spirits. Spirituality is something I am passionate about, and I believe my purpose is to help people by sharing my story, in order to help others grow spiritually, and to live their best life despite their financial situation. At the time of writing this book, I am 56 years old and have just discovered my true passion and purpose. It may take time, but you will find yours too. The fact that you are reading this now tells me you are closer to achieving your goal of finding your passion and purpose sooner than you realize.

So, what is passion and purpose? Passion is something that makes you happy, fulfilled, and energized when you are doing it. When you are passionate, you lose all track of time and get lost in the project. It is fun. Purpose is something you are meant to do; it is your calling. When you find your passion and purpose, you wake up early to start your day and go to bed reluctantly because you want to continue with your purpose. That is my definition of passion.

Why is discovering your passion and purpose so important? It is the unique way we follow our path. When we are passionate, we become enthusiastic about life and more resilient. We can overcome obstacles better. Working for money alone can be draining on our soul, leading to depression and going to work just for the sake of the money. When we add passion to the formula, everything becomes possible. We become magical.

How do we find our passion and purpose? First and foremost, we must discover what motivates us. What are your likes and dislikes? What are your common interests and hobbies? For me, I discovered through my numerology as a master number 22 that I am a builder; I love to create something. I love organization and the ability to start something from the ground up. This is why I love to write—it is about building an entire book that wasn't there before. Find what you are passionate about by diving deep into your likes and dislikes.

Spirituality, such as tarot reading, has always been a passion of mine, although I didn't always give it the attention it deserved. Instead, I often let it take a backseat, practicing it sporadically whenever I found the time. Understanding your own interests and hobbies can be a crucial step in discovering your passion and purpose. What activities do you find yourself drawn to, even in your spare time? What talents and skills do you possess that come naturally to you?

One effective method to uncover your passion and purpose is to seek feedback from those around you—family, colleagues, and friends. They can provide valuable insight into your strengths and weaknesses, highlighting aspects of yourself that you may not fully recognize. This outside perspective can illuminate potential paths or interests that resonate deeply with you but have been overlooked or undervalued.

Exploring these interests and talents through introspection and external feedback can lead you closer to identifying activities and pursuits that ignite a sense of fulfillment and purpose in your life. It's a journey of self-discovery that involves both looking inward and seeking external perspectives to align your passions with your life's purpose.

What I've discovered from reading biographies of famous individuals is that their journeys in discovering passion and purpose can serve as profound motivation for anyone. Consider exploring the lives of Steve Jobs, who revolutionized technology, Nelson Mandela, whose fight for justice inspired the world, Elvis Presley, who transformed music and entertainment, and Mother Teresa, whose compassion touched countless lives. Each of these figures found their calling through perseverance and self-discovery. Albert Einstein, with his quest for understanding the universe, and many others like them, offers valuable insight into how passion can shape our lives. Who resonates with you? Dive into their stories, uncover the paths they took, and begin to unravel your own journey toward passion and purpose.

One of the exercises in the reflective exercise section encourages you to write about your ideal day. When I did this exercise, I discovered that my ideal day closely resembles my daily life. With just a few minor adjustments, I realized that I am living a life filled with passion, purpose, and alignment to who I truly am. That is my *Soulful Minimalism*: a life filled with passion on less.

Reflective Exercises:

1. What activities did you enjoy the most as a child? Why did you love

them?

Reflect on your childhood and list the activities that brought you the most joy. Consider why these activities were so meaningful to you. What aspects of them sparked your enthusiasm and excitement?

1. What did you dream of becoming when you were young?

Think back to your childhood dreams and aspirations. What did you imagine yourself doing as an adult? How do these dreams align with your current interests and passions?

1. What hobbies or activities do you currently enjoy?

Identify the hobbies and activities that you find fulfilling today. What about them makes you happy? How do they contribute to your sense of purpose and well-being?

1. Describe a day when you felt particularly fulfilled and content. What were you doing?

Recall a specific day when you felt a deep sense of fulfillment and contentment. What activities were you engaged in? What made that day so special and meaningful to you?

1. List the activities you do daily. Which ones bring you joy, and which feel like chores?

Make a list of your daily activities and categorize them based on how they make you feel. Reflect on why certain activities bring you joy and why others feel burdensome.

1. Are there any tasks or activities that make you lose track of time? What are they?

Identify activities that fully absorb your attention and make you lose track of time. These are often clues to your passions and interests that align with your life's purpose.

1. Think about moments when you felt truly inspired. What were you doing? Who were you with?

1. Reflect on times when you felt a surge of inspiration. What were you doing during these moments? Who were you with? How can you incorporate more of these inspiring experiences into your life?

1. What books, movies, or topics do you find yourself drawn to repeatedly?

Consider the books, movies, and topics that you are consistently drawn to. What themes or subjects resonate with you? How do they connect to your interests and passions?

1. What causes or issues do you feel passionately about?

Identify the causes or issues that ignite your passion and concern. How can you contribute to these areas in a way that aligns with your values and purpose?

1. What values are most important to you, and how do they influence your interests?

Reflect on your core values and how they shape your interests and choices. How do these values guide you in pursuing activities and goals that are meaningful to you?

1. List your top five skills or talents.

Identify your top five skills or talents. How can you leverage these strengths to pursue your passions and contribute to your sense of purpose?

SOULFUL MINIMALISM

1. Spend 10 minutes writing down all the activities you enjoy or have enjoyed in the past. Don't censor yourself; just write whatever comes to mind.

Set a timer for 10 minutes and list all the activities you enjoy or have enjoyed in the past. Let your thoughts flow freely without judgment. Review your list and identify common themes or patterns.

1. Create a dream/ manifestation board (physical or digital) that represents your passions and interests. Include images, words, and quotes that inspire you and reflect your ideal life. Use this dream board as a visual reminder of what you love.

Gather images, words, and quotes that resonate with your passions and interests. Arrange them on a board to create a visual representation of your ideal life. Display your dream board in a place where you can see it daily for inspiration and motivation.

1. Creating your ideal day: What would your ideal day look like? What would you do? Where would you go? Who is with you? Create this in your journal and write for 5 minutes. Set the timer and write without putting too much thought into it. Just start writing and be creative.

Envision your perfect day and describe it in detail in your journal. Write about what you would do, where you would go, and who would be with you. Allow yourself to dream and be creative without overthinking. This exercise can reveal important insight into what you truly desire in life.

> *"The only way to do great work is to love what you do."*
> —Steve Jobs

Chapter Nine: Navigating Your Journey—Goals and Values

Welcome to the next phase of creating passionate living with less. At the heart of living a passionate life lies a profound understanding of your core values, your destination, and the goals you wish to achieve. For me, identifying my core values—education, freedom, self-improvement, love, empathy, gratitude, authenticity, and compassion—has been pivotal. These values form the bedrock of my existence, guiding every decision and action I take. To take a deeper look into core values and goal setting check out my book *Beyond the Canvas: Create your dream life with vision boards*. This guided journal comes with worksheets to help you expand on your goals setting and values journey.

I have always had a passion for building and expanding who I am on a core, deep level. Goal setting has always intrigued me, and I have taken multiple courses on the subject. Each course offered its unique perspective on how to set goals. In my book *Beyond the Canvas*, I created my own concept of goal setting, which I will share a glimpse of here in this chapter of *Soulful Minimalism* because this book would not be complete without it.

As I researched the concepts of values and goal setting, I developed my own approach. When I first started my book *Beyond the Canvas*, it had a different name, and I showcased it to my Vision Board students. Their reactions were very appreciative because the book helped clarify, simplify, and make the process of creating a vision board seamless. People create vision boards all the time, but the simple fact is, it's not that simple. If you just want something to look at and dream about, that's fine. But I wanted to create a vision board that actually worked. So I studied vision boarding, took several courses, and received a certificate on facilitating vision board workshops.

In Chapter Eight, I guided you through creating a dream board—a space where anything is possible and where your wildest dreams take shape. If you've created one, that's fantastic! As we conclude the final chapter, you'll have the opportunity to create a vision board, allowing you to see the subtle yet powerful difference between the two. A dream board is like a manifestation board, capturing the limitless possibilities of the life you dream of living. A vision board, however, is a visual goal board— a focused tool designed to help you manifest your true desires with intention and clarity, mapping out the steps to turn your dreams into reality. This is my unique approach to working with both dream and vision boards, each serving a distinct purpose on your journey.

The trick to a successful vision board is knowing what you want, which is often easier said than done. This clarity doesn't come overnight; it needs to be nourished, cultivated, and continually worked on. In *Beyond the Canvas*, we delve deeply into this process. But for now, let's focus on the heart of a good vision board: the goals you aim to achieve.

What do you want out of life? How does one uncover their true desires and ambitions? Understanding your goals and values is essential for navigating your life with purpose. This chapter will help you explore these questions, providing you with the tools to create a vision board that aligns with your deepest aspirations.

In one of my vision board facilitator classes, we were asked to write our own obituary. This assignment aimed to make us think about how we want our lives to be. How do we want to be recognized? Who do we want to become? What do we want to accomplish? And so on. I energetically did the assignment and came up with this:

Obituary of Karen Rose Kobylka

Karen Rose Kobylka, a radiant soul who embraced the spiritual journey with grace and fervor, has peacefully transitioned into the realm beyond the physical. Born with a deep understanding of the continuity of existence, Karen believed in the enduring presence of the spirit long after the body fades away.

Unbeknownst to many, Karen was not only a beloved friend and family member but also a gifted medium. Her connection to the spiritual realm was nurtured by her mother, herself a medium, who shared tales of spiritual encounters and provided unwavering support as Karen navigated her own spiritual awakening. Though she initially veiled this aspect of herself, it was through the passing of her mother that Karen fully embraced her role as a conduit between the physical and spiritual worlds.

KAREN ROSE KOBYLKA

Karen embarked on a journey of self-discovery and spiritual growth. Her training as a medium in Vancouver Island, Canada, allowed her to harness her innate gifts and serve as a beacon of light for those seeking connection and solace beyond the veil.

In the words of Prince, who she now joins in the afterworld, Karen believed in a realm of never-ending happiness, where the sun shines eternally, illuminating the path for all who have crossed over. While her physical presence may be no more, her spirit lives on, casting its gentle light upon those she loved and cherished.

Karen leaves behind cherished memories and an indelible legacy of love, kindness, and spiritual insight. As we mourn her physical absence, let us take comfort in knowing that she continues to watch over us, guiding us through life's journey with the same compassion and wisdom that defined her time on earth.

In lieu of flowers, the family requests donations be made to (Mental Health/Bipolar Disorder Charity) *in Karen's memory, honoring her commitment to spreading love and light in the world.*

A celebration of Karen's life will be held at [details later], where friends and loved ones will gather to commemorate her remarkable journey and the profound impact she had on all who were fortunate enough to know her. Though she may have departed this world, her spirit remains ever-present, a testament to the enduring power of love and the eternal nature of the soul.

The assignment made me reflect on my values and goals. It empowered me to live a better life so that, when it is time for my life to come to an end, it will be a life full of aspirations, dreams, and goals fulfilled.

Understanding your core values is like having a compass that directs your life's journey. They represent what matters most to you, reflecting the principles and beliefs that define who you are and how you navigate the world. They serve as a lens through which you assess opportunities, make choices, and align your actions with your deepest aspirations.

Once you clarify your core values, the next step is defining your goals—those milestones and achievements that resonate with your values and bring meaning to your life. Goals give shape to your aspirations, providing a roadmap towards personal fulfillment and purposeful living. They range from short-term objectives to long-term visions, each contributing to the larger tapestry of your journey. By aligning your goals with your values, you cultivate a life that is not only purpose driven but also deeply satisfying on a soulful level.

What are your Core Values?

Identifying your core values is essential, as they serve as powerful motivators in your life. The clearer and more defined your core values, the greater alignment you can achieve while creating your dream life. Core values are often referred to as personal values.

How Understanding Values Will Help You:

Values play a significant role in our lives, whether we consciously recognize them or not. Acknowledging and honoring our values can simplify decision-making and planning. For example, if you value family but your job demands a 50-hour work week, this misalignment may lead to conflict and stress. A solid understanding of our values empowers us to make life decisions confidently. It guides us in answering crucial questions like:

- Should I leave my job?
- Should I accept this job promotion?
- Should I compromise my standards?
- Should I start my own business?
- Should I follow tradition or explore a new path in life?

Comprehending our values helps us navigate life's complexities and make choices that resonate with our true priorities.

How Would You Define Your Values?

To answer this question, we must first grasp a clear understanding of what values represent. Values are the principles we deem important in how we lead our lives. Ideally, they dictate our life priorities and serve as benchmarks to assess if our lives are progressing in the desired direction. Identifying our values is a crucial step in understanding what we genuinely want from life.

Defining your core values:

Check off your core beliefs and add to them as needed.

- Accountability
- Achievement
- Adventurousness
- Authenticity
- Ambition
- Assertiveness
- Balance
- Belonging
- Boldness
- Carefulness
- Calmness
- Clear Mindedness
- Community
- Compassion
- Connection
- Consistency
- Contentment
- Self Improvement
- Determination
- Love
- Loyalty
- Dependability
- Devoutness
- Diligence
- Discipline
- Diversity
- Effectiveness
- Efficiency
- Empathy
- Enthusiasm
- Equality
- Excellence
- Excitement

- Exploration
- Expressiveness
- Fairness
- Faith
- Freedom
- Generosity
- Goodness
- Giving
- Growth
- Hard Work
- Giving
- Honesty
- Hope
- Independence
- Ingenuity
- Identity
- Justice
- Leadership
- Legacy
- Loyalty
- Openness
- Practicality
- Purpose
- Professionalism
- Progress
- Reliability
- Resourcefulness
- Relationships
- Security
- Stability

Goal Setting 101:

- Decide What You Want: Clearly define your aspirations. What are the specific outcomes you desire? Be precise and detailed in outlining

your goals.
- Believe You Can Achieve It: Cultivate a deep belief in your ability to attain your goals. This positive mindset is a driving force behind the success of achieving your goals.
- Plan for Success: Develop a strategic plan to accomplish your goals. Break down larger objectives into manageable steps, creating a roadmap to guide your journey.
- Stay Motivated: Sustain your enthusiasm and motivation throughout the journey. Regularly revisit your goals, celebrate small victories, and adjust your plan as needed to stay on course.

Remember, effective goal setting sets the stage for a dream life. One that truly inspires and guides you toward the life you envision.

I have always been passionate about setting goals and creating vision boards my entire life. Some goals I would achieve, other goals I would not. The trick is to know yourself on a deep level so that you can create a dream life for yourself. By becoming clear on what you want, you can then have a road map for yourself and your life.

Self-Enhancement Goals:

Self-enhancement goals form the essence of personal development, encompassing a diverse spectrum across physical, emotional, spiritual, and social dimensions. These goals are your personal roadmap for growth, embracing a myriad of possibilities. They could involve honing specific skills, both personally and professionally, embarking on meaningful endeavors, conquering fears that have held you back, pursuing career milestones, or even delving into creative pursuits that ignite your passion. Whether it's developing new abilities, achieving personal milestones, cultivating a fulfilling social life, or finding inner peace, self-enhancement goals are the threads that weave the fabric of your unique journey. They represent the conscious choices you make to evolve into the best version of yourself, guiding you toward a life rich in fulfillment and purpose. So, as you embark on the journey of self-enhancement, consider the vast tapestry of possibilities that these goals present, each thread contributing to the masterpiece that is your life.

Examples of Self Enhancement Goals:

SOULFUL MINIMALISM

Physical:

- Achieve a specific fitness milestone, such as running a marathon or mastering a new yoga pose.
- Adopt a healthier lifestyle by incorporating regular exercise and balanced nutrition.
- Improve overall well-being by getting adequate sleep and managing stress.

Emotional:

- Develop resilience in the face of challenges and setbacks.
- Cultivate a positive mindset through daily gratitude practices.
- Work on enhancing emotional intelligence to navigate relationships more effectively.

Spiritual:

- Establish a consistent meditation or mindfulness practice.
- Explore and deepen personal spiritual beliefs or practices.
- Engage in activities that foster a sense of connection with something greater than oneself.

Social:

- Expand social circles by attending networking events or joining clubs.
- Improve communication skills to build stronger connections with others.
- Actively seek out and nurture meaningful relationships.

Skills Development:

- Acquire a new language or improve proficiency in an existing one.
- Pursue a certification or additional education to enhance professional skills.
- Learn a new instrument, art form, or any skill aligned with personal

interests.

Career:

- Set clear career advancement goals, such as securing a promotion or leadership role.
- Develop a strategic plan for professional growth and skill enhancement.
- Explore entrepreneurship or new career paths aligned with passions.

Conquering Fears:

- Face and overcome specific fears, whether public speaking or confronting personal phobias.
- Gradually step out of comfort zones to build confidence.
- Challenge limiting beliefs that hinder personal or professional growth.

Creative Pursuits:

- Start a creative project, such as writing a book, painting, or composing music.
- Explore different artistic expressions to find a creative outlet.
- Join a creative community to share and collaborate on artistic endeavors.

Remember, these examples are just a starting point, and self-enhancement goals can be tailored to individual preferences, values, and aspirations. They serve as personalized milestones guiding you towards a more fulfilling and purposeful life.

Pinnacle Pursuits Goals:

Embark on a journey of self-discovery and growth as you delve into your Pinnacle Pursuits. These are not just goals; they are the manifestations of your deepest desires—gateways to a whole new level of pleasure, passion, and personal evolution. In this section, explore the experiences you want to live, the achievements you wish to accomplish, the tangible items you dream to

SOULFUL MINIMALISM

have, and the creative endeavors you aspire to do. These are the elements that will elevate your existence and set the stage for boundless growth. Dream big and let your Pinnacle Pursuits guide you toward a life rich in fulfillment and accomplishment.

Examples of Pinnacle Pursuits:

Experiences to Live:

- Embark on a luxurious cruise to exotic destinations.
- Skydive over breathtaking landscapes for an adrenaline-fueled adventure.
- Set foot on every continent during a globe-trotting expedition.
- Immerse yourself in the rich culture of far-off lands on a world tour.

Achievements to Accomplish:

- Launch a passion project or business that aligns with your values.
- Attain a professional or personal milestone that signifies growth.
- Complete a challenging fitness or wellness goal for a sense of accomplishment.
- Earn a certification or degree to enhance your skills and expertise.

Tangible Items to Have:

- Acquire a dream car that reflects your style and aspirations.
- Invest in a beautiful home, whether it's a cozy retreat or a mansion in a sought-after location.
- Own artwork, antiques, or items that bring joy and aesthetic pleasure.
- Cultivate a collection that holds sentimental or historic value.

Creative Endeavors to Do:

- Write and publish a book that shares your unique perspective.
- Create and exhibit art that resonates with your creative expression.
- Compose and perform music that brings joy to yourself and others.

Wealth Goals:

Embark on a journey to create wealth that transcends financial prosperity, taking you to new heights of passion, pleasure, and personal growth. Consider the level of abundance you aspire to, the security you envision, and the transformative impact wealth can have on your life. Envision the lifestyle you wish to create, making your goals so vivid that they feel within reach. Picture yourself like a child on Christmas Eve, with limitless possibilities awaiting.

Wealth Goals may include:

- Investment Goals: Strategize and plan investments that align with your financial aspirations.
- Savings: Establish savings plans to ensure financial security and achieve your wealth objectives.
- Financial Endeavors: Explore any financial initiatives that contribute to your wealth-building journey.
- Retirement Planning: Secure your future by outlining goals related to retirement and financial stability.

This section invites you to dream big, considering not just the monetary aspects but also the holistic wealth that enriches your life. Visualize the abundance you desire, making these goals so tangible that they feel like present realities. Your vision board becomes a canvas for manifesting wealth and prosperity, where the sky is truly the limit.

Reflective Exercises:

1. Identify Your Top Eight Values

- Take a moment to reflect on what is truly important to you. Write down your top eight values in your journal. Consider aspects like family, health, personal growth, creativity, financial stability, adventure, spirituality, and service to others.

2. Rapid Writing for Goal Categories

- Set a timer for five minutes. During this time, write as quickly as you can about your self-enhancement goals. These could include areas like personal development, education, and physical health. Repeat this process for your Pinnacle Pursuits goals (aspirational achievements that bring you the highest satisfaction) and your wealth goals (financial objectives and milestones). The key is to capture as many ideas as possible without overthinking.

3. Prioritize Your Goals

- Review the goals you've listed in each category from the previous exercise. Select the top three goals for each category. These should be the goals that resonate most deeply with you and align with your values. Write these top goals in your journal.

4. Develop Action Plans

- For each of your top goals, create a detailed action plan. Break down each goal into smaller, manageable steps. Consider the resources you will need, potential obstacles, and strategies to overcome them. Write these action plans in your journal, outlining the steps you will take, the timeline for each step, and how you will measure your progress.

5. Writing Your Obituary

- Purpose: This exercise is designed to help you uncover what truly matters to you by imagining how you want to be remembered. It can clarify your passions, purpose, goals, and values, guiding you toward a more meaningful and fulfilling life.

Instructions:

Find a quiet, comfortable place where you won't be disturbed. Take a few moments to relax.

Reflect on Your Life: Close your eyes and visualize the life you want to lead. Think about the achievements, relationships, and contributions you hope to be remembered for.

Begin Writing: Start writing your obituary as if it were to be published in a newspaper or shared at a memorial service. Include the following elements:

Introduction: Begin with basic information such as your name, date of birth, and date of passing (you can leave this blank or use a distant future date).

Life Overview: Summarize your life's journey. Highlight significant milestones, accomplishments, and experiences. Think about the moments that defined you.

Passions and Interests: Describe the passions and interests that brought you joy and fulfillment. What activities or hobbies were you known for? How did you pursue these interests?

Purpose and Contributions: Reflect on your life's purpose. What were the causes or issues you were passionate about? How did you make a difference in the world? Mention any volunteer work, community involvement, or personal projects that were important to you.

Relationships and Legacy: Write about the relationships that mattered most to you. How did you impact the lives of your family, friends, and community? What legacy do you want to leave behind?

Review and Reflect: Once you've finished writing, read through your obituary. Reflect on what you've written and consider the following questions:

Passions and Purpose: What passions and purposes stand out? How can you incorporate more of these into your current life?

Goals and Values: What goals and values are evident in your obituary? How do they align with your current goals and values?

Are there changes you need to make to better align your life with your true passions and purpose?

Action Steps: Based on your reflections, identify specific actions you can take to move closer to the life you envisioned. Write these actions down and create a plan to implement them.

By writing your obituary, you gain a unique perspective on your life, helping you to focus on what truly matters. Use this exercise to guide your journey toward living a life aligned with your deepest passions, purpose, goals, and values.

> *"You are never too old to set another goal or to dream a new dream."*
> –C.S. Lewis

Chapter Ten: Educate to Elevate - Building a Fulfilling Life

One of my passions is learning. I love to learn something new every day. I strive to be better than the woman in the obituary I wrote. I want to list my achievements and create world-renowned charities to help people lead better lives. I understand how difficult life can be, but I also know how much we can improve our lives if we motivate ourselves and advance our skills. If we stay motivated long enough and aim for greatness, we can change not only our world but also the worlds of those around us. This is why I love taking courses and learning new things. It feeds my soul and puts me back in control of my life. I know what it's like to lose control.

As of my last count, I have completed over 250 online courses. These range from certified meditation teacher, certified Law of Attraction coach, as well as soul coaching and life coaching, counseling, tarot reading, personal development, and much more. My journey into online learning began after writing *Soul Dance*. I was determined to improve my life, even while on welfare and later, disability. I knew I had to rebuild after my brain health issues disrupted my life. Following my soul's guidance, I realized that rebuilding my beauty empire was no longer my passion—it had served its purpose. I had lost all my contacts, staff, and associates due to my brain health issues. Instead, my soul told me to advance my skill set so I could guide others into greatness.

I remember when I was on welfare—it was a very difficult time, to say the least. After I got out of the hospital, I ended up in a rooming house with just my suitcase and no television. I had my phone, so I started watching YouTube. When I wasn't writing my story of *Soul Dance*, I immersed myself in YouTube videos. I listened to Abraham-Hicks on the Law of Attraction, learning how to manifest and create abundance in my life. I also watched videos on the Tao Te Ching, a Chinese philosophy by Lao Tzu. The Tao Te Ching is essentially a how-to guide for creating harmony within yourself and the world around you. This knowledge prevented me from attempting to end my life again. The more I studied, the more empowered I became to live my life. YouTube saved my life.

Soon after, I started taking online courses whenever they went on sale. Little by little, I purchased courses on spirituality, which truly saved me. I had always studied spiritual courses back in my hometown before moving to Vancouver Island. I delved into mediumship, tarot, numerology, the Law of Attraction, reiki, and spiritual healing at least three days a week. Even after moving to the Island, I continued my studies until my brain health issues interrupted my life. Learning has always been a pivotal part of my life.

My passion for education didn't start with spirituality, though. Reflecting on my life, I remember how my mother would buy me books as soon as I could read. I loved books. As I got older, I wanted to be a makeup artist and hairstylist. I attended beauty school to become a journeyman hairstylist, barber, and beautician. Later, I became an esthetician and makeup artist for the stars. I also studied business and marketing through local colleges and became a keynote speaker at provincial beauty trade shows, teaching people how to be the best makeup artists they could be.

My passion for education didn't end there. I worked at the brilliant Estelle Academy of Hair Design as a hairstylist and makeup artist instructor. Soon after, I developed my own makeup academy in my beautiful 5000 square-foot salon and spa headquarters. Education has always been a passion of mine. It feeds my soul and makes my heart sing.

I firmly believe that anything is possible if you put your mind to it. Statistically, the chances of me escaping poverty are slim, but every morning, I wake up and give it my best shot, doing it all with passion. Learning has become fun and joyous for me. It helps me focus on positive growth rather than my current challenges of a limited income and a small circle of friends. It feeds my soul and gives me purpose.

While I may not be able to afford top-notch colleges or universities, I've found invaluable knowledge through these online courses. I also devour audiobooks, gaining insights from gems of information available not only from online stores like Audible but also from local libraries for free.

The benefits of lifelong learning are immense. It boosts self-esteem, provides a sense of purpose, and fosters growth from the inside out. Additionally, it keeps the mind sharp and engaged, paving the way to a fulfilling life, regardless of financial constraints.

When you immerse yourself in learning, you open up new worlds of possibilities. Each new piece of knowledge, each skill acquired, adds another layer to your understanding and capability. It's like adding tools to a toolbox, equipping yourself to handle life's challenges more effectively and creatively.

For those of us living with less, education becomes a beacon of hope. It's a reminder that no matter our financial situation, we have the power to enrich our minds and expand our horizons. Whether through free online courses, public libraries, or community resources, there are numerous ways to continue learning and growing without breaking the bank.

Consider setting aside time each day for learning. It could be as simple as listening to an audiobook during your commute, enrolling in a free online course, or reading articles on topics that interest you. The key is to make learning a regular part of your routine.

Learning doesn't have to be a solitary endeavor. Join study groups, participate in online forums, or engage in community education classes. Sharing knowledge and learning with others can be incredibly motivating and enriching.

Remember, lifelong learning is not just about acquiring new information; it's about nurturing curiosity and a love for discovery. It's about staying mentally active and open to new ideas, which in turn fosters resilience and adaptability. These qualities are crucial for anyone striving to live passionately and purposefully, especially when resources are limited.

Embrace the power of knowledge as a fundamental component of passionate living. It can transform your life, boost your confidence, and provide the tools you need to navigate your journey with grace and determination. Keep learning, keep growing, and let your thirst for knowledge light the path to a more fulfilling life.

Exploring Online Learning and Financial Aid

There are massive amounts of online courses to choose from. Some I have used, and others I have not. To get you started, here is a list of online academies available to choose from: Coursera, Udemy, edX, Khan Academy, Center of Excellence, New Skills Academy and Mind Valley. These are just some of the platforms. I urge you to go ahead and start your own research on what and where you would like to study. Remember that libraries are a wealth of knowledge and often hold classes on a variety of subjects. When doing your research, there are often scholarship opportunities that become available through various academies and smaller online courses.

SOULFUL MINIMALISM

One of the greatest barriers to formal education for many people is the cost. However, numerous scholarship opportunities and financial aid options can make higher education more accessible, even for those with limited financial resources. Here are some avenues to explore:

1. Government Grants and Scholarships:

- In many countries, governments offer grants and scholarships based on financial need, academic merit, or specific fields of study.
- International scholarships are also available for those looking to study abroad, with numerous countries offering scholarships to attract international students.

1. Institutional Scholarships:

- Many universities offer scholarships to attract talented students. These can be based on academic performance, athletic ability, artistic talent, or other criteria. Research the universities you're interested in to find out what scholarships they offer.

1. Nonprofit and Corporate Scholarships:

- Many nonprofit organizations offer scholarships to support students from specific backgrounds, communities, or fields of study.
- Large corporations often offer scholarships as part of their corporate social responsibility programs.

1. Online Scholarship Databases:

- Websites like Fastweb, Scholarships.com, and Cappex offer comprehensive databases of scholarships. These platforms allow you to create profiles and receive personalized lists of scholarships for which you may be eligible.

By exploring these opportunities and leveraging available resources, you can make formal education more affordable and attainable. Education is a powerful tool for personal and professional growth, and financial constraints should not stand in the way of pursuing your dreams.

Leveraging Knowledge for Personal Growth

I suggest setting your schedule and committing to at least 30 minutes a day to education. This will get you into a routine and expand your awareness of how great you can become. I have a lot of time on my hands, so I dedicate five to ten hours per day to self-study. It's not formal study, but it's all I can afford, so I do the best with what I have.

Before I moved into my current space, I had very little room to work with. It proved to be very challenging with my previous roommate. When she was home, it was loud and eventful, limiting the space and time I had for study. I made the most of the quieter moments when she was away working, studying as long as I could.

Now, I have a small office space to myself, allowing me to utilize my time better. My new home is tranquil, with my desk and computer overlooking a grassy knoll with trees and a forest. It's beautiful and very spiritual. I often see wild rabbits and many different types of birds outside my window. It's a wonderful space to create and learn from.

I urge you to make the best of your current situation, no matter how small. If your space is limited, add a plant or some flowers to brighten it up. Declutter, organize, and create a tranquil environment that encourages productivity and growth. If you live with roommates, family, or friends, have a chat with them about your goals so they can support you and give you the space you need when necessary.

Creating a conducive environment for learning is crucial, and sometimes it takes a bit of creativity and communication to achieve that. Remember, it's not about having the perfect space; it's about making the best of what you have and staying committed to your personal growth.

The journey of expanding your knowledge and learning new skills is often filled with obstacles. Recognizing these challenges and finding ways to overcome them is essential for your success. One of the most common obstacles is finding the time to dedicate to learning. To overcome this, try breaking your study sessions into smaller chunks. Even dedicating just 30 minutes a day will work wonders for you and your education. Use tools like calendars or apps to schedule and remind you of your study sessions.

SOULFUL MINIMALISM

In our digital age, distractions are everywhere. Create a dedicated study space where you can focus without interruptions. Turn off notifications on your devices, and if possible, inform those around you of your study times so they can respect your need for quiet.

It's easy to put off studying, especially when the material feels overwhelming. Combat procrastination by setting clear, achievable goals. Find ways to keep your enthusiasm high, such as studying topics you are passionate about or connecting with others who share your interests.

Maintaining motivation throughout your learning journey is crucial. Here are some techniques to help keep your spirits high: Break down your learning objectives into smaller, more manageable goals. Achieving these smaller milestones can give you a sense of accomplishment and keep you motivated to continue. Reward yourself when you reach a significant milestone. Whether it's treating yourself to a favorite snack, taking a break, or doing something you enjoy, celebrating your achievements can boost your morale and keep you motivated. Keep a journal. Seeing how far you've come can be incredibly motivating and provide a clear record of your accomplishments.

Engaging with others who share your passion can provide support, encouragement, and new perspectives. Cultivate a mindset of curiosity and exploration. Approach your learning with a sense of wonder and excitement.

Learning is a marathon, not a sprint. It's important to cultivate patience and persistence to see long-term success. Realize that mastering new skills or knowledge takes time. Be patient with yourself and recognize that setbacks and mistakes are part of the learning process. A growth mindset helps you stay resilient in the face of difficulties and encourages continuous improvement. It's better to study regularly for shorter periods than to cram intensely for long sessions. Consistent, steady progress leads to better retention and less burnout. Everyone experiences obstacles and failures. Use these moments as learning opportunities rather than reasons to give up. Keep your long-term goals in mind. Remind yourself why you started this journey and what you hope to achieve. This vision can keep you grounded and focused during challenging times.

By acknowledging and addressing common obstacles, staying motivated, and cultivating patience and persistence, you can successfully navigate your learning journey and unlock your full potential.

What I love most about online learning is the flexibility it offers—you can work at your own pace. Most courses provide lifetime access, allowing you to revisit the material whenever you need a refresher. This is particularly valuable as you grow and expand your knowledge. You can always go back and review concepts to ensure you fully grasp them.

Knowledge has become a passion of mine. It gives me a sense of control over my life, especially when circumstances have taken that control away. The ability to grow and transform through learning is empowering. It provides me with a purpose and a reason to keep striving. My passion for gaining knowledge fuels my journey to become a spiritual soul coach, helping others who are struggling to become the best versions of themselves.

My goal in writing this book is to inspire you. No matter what your financial situation is, you can live a life filled with passion and purpose. I hope that the pages you've read so far have ignited a spark within you. Embrace the power of learning and let it guide you toward a fulfilling and meaningful life.

Reflective Exercises:
1: Developing an Action Plan

- Creating a step-by-step action plan ensures systematic learning and progress towards your educational goals.
- Instructions:
    A. Break Down Learning: Divide your learning objectives into manageable tasks. Outline specific steps you need to take to acquire each piece of knowledge or skill.
    B. Set Deadlines: Assign realistic deadlines to each task. This helps maintain momentum and ensures steady progress.
    C. Implementation: Consider how and when you will engage with each resource. Schedule study sessions, set aside time for coursework, or plan meetings with mentors.
        - Example: If one of your goals is to learn a new programming language, your action plan might include weekly online tutorials, practicing coding exercises daily, and completing a small project within a month.

SOULFUL MINIMALISM

2: Reflecting on Personal Growth

- Reflecting on how acquiring new knowledge contributes to personal growth and well-being reinforces the significance of your learning journey.
- Instructions:

A. Align with Core Values: Consider how the knowledge you seek aligns with your core values and life purpose. Reflect on the impact it will have on your personal development and overall happiness.
B. Long-Term Benefits: Explore how acquiring this knowledge will benefit your career, relationships, or personal interests. Visualize the positive outcomes of mastering new skills.
    - Example: Learning about mindfulness techniques aligns with a core value of personal well-being and may lead to reduced stress levels and improved mental clarity.

3: Staying Motivated

- Establishing strategies to stay motivated ensures consistency and perseverance throughout your learning journey.
- Instructions:
    A. Set Milestones: Break your learning process into smaller milestones. Celebrate achievements when you reach these milestones to maintain enthusiasm.
    B. Seek Support: Share your learning goals with friends, family, or a supportive community. Seek encouragement and advice when facing challenges.
    C. Adapt and Adjust: Stay flexible and adjust your plan as needed. Recognize and overcome obstacles with resilience and determination.
        - Example: Joining an online study group or attending webinars related to your field of interest can provide ongoing motivation and a sense of community.

By thoroughly reflecting on these points, you can create a clear and actionable roadmap to achieve your goals. Remember, learning is a lifelong journey, and each step you take brings you closer to living a passionate and fulfilling life.

"I don't care how much power, brilliance or energy you have, if you don't harness it and focus it on a specific target, and hold it there, you're never going to accomplish as much as your ability warrants."
— Zig Ziglar

Chapter Eleven: Guided Growth: The Power of Mentorship

Before diving into the details of mentorship, let's first clarify what a mentor truly represents. In my view, a mentor is someone who possesses greater knowledge and skill than oneself and is willing to share that expertise to aid in personal growth and learning. In my own journey, I've been fortunate to have had a mentor who was a renowned spiritual medium. Their guidance and teachings were instrumental during a significant period of my life, chronicled in my book *Soul Dance*. Unfortunately, due to challenges with my brain health, I eventually had to navigate without an official mentor.

Despite this, I've found inspiration and guidance from various figures who have impacted my path to success. One such individual is Sheetal, a friend who, despite our diverging paths, continues to serve as an unofficial mentor. Her dedication to education and business growth has been a beacon of motivation for me. Additionally, I've looked up to my eldest sister, who leads a remarkably successful life and serves as a role model for me in many aspects.

Mentorship thrives prominently in structured environments like business, where employees often benefit from the wisdom and experience of long-term colleagues. Some organizations even establish formal mentorship programs to facilitate these relationships and enhance professional development.

The essence of mentorship lies in its ability to elevate individuals to new levels of education and understanding. It provides invaluable guidance that can steer one toward achieving higher aspirations and personal fulfillment. As we explore further, we'll delve into the mechanics of finding and fostering meaningful mentorship relationships that can shape our journeys for the better.

When I was young, I grew up with three older siblings who were ten plus years older than I. As I got older, I found myself always looking up to them and naturally gravitating towards older friends who became my mentors. This approach to life was instinctive for me and proved to be a catalyst for growth and discovery. In my book *Soul Dance*, I discuss my journey with my mentor and spiritual minister Harry. Harry was the person who eventually charged me with criminal harassment when I had my brain health issues, and I considered him my mentor. Losing that relationship was a great challenge, and sometimes I still feel sad when I think about how it ended.

Harry was an expert in his field, and attending his courses was an exhilarating experience for me. Back then, I had the financial means to take courses from upscale educational institutions like his. Finding a mentor when you have money is relatively easy, and losing that mentorship was a loss I grieved deeply. I have yet to find an equal or better mentor, so I do my best to read books and to carry on.

In the absence of a direct mentor, I have found inspiration in celebrity personal development experts like Esther Hicks from Abraham Hicks and Michael Bernard Beckwith, a minister and author featured in the movie *The Secret*. These individuals have become my unofficial mentors, providing guidance and wisdom through their teachings. Although they are unaware of their impact on me, I consider them mentors because of the profound influence they've had on my personal growth. Having such figures to look up to can propel you to new heights if you dedicate yourself to personal growth.

The key to finding a mentor is to choose someone in a field you are passionate about. This is a catalyst for passionate living. If you work or have a career, having a mentor within your organization is crucial to the growth of both the establishment and your career.

Mentorship is a dynamic relationship where a more experienced individual guides and supports someone less experienced to enhance their personal and professional growth. It involves sharing knowledge, insights, and advice to help the mentee navigate challenges and achieve their goals. Mentorship encompasses more than just teaching or advising; it involves a deep commitment to the mentee's development. A mentor provides guidance, constructive feedback, and encouragement based on their own experiences and expertise. It is not about controlling or directing the mentee's path but rather empowering them to make informed decisions.

Formal mentors are often part of structured programs or professional relationships where mentorship is a defined role. These mentors may be assigned or chosen based on specific criteria. Informal mentors develop naturally through personal connections or relationships where mutual respect and trust evolve over time. Personal mentors offer guidance in personal growth, life decisions, and overall well-being. They may include family members, friends, or individuals with whom there is a deep personal connection. Professional mentors focus on career development, skill enhancement, and navigating professional challenges. They often come from within one's field or industry and provide insight into career progression and industry trends.

Mentors can help mentees build self-confidence, improve self-awareness, and develop a clearer sense of personal identity and goals. Mentors share practical knowledge and expertise, helping mentees acquire new skills and refine existing ones. This can accelerate professional growth and enhance job performance. Mentors often open doors to valuable networks and connections within their field or industry, providing access to new opportunities, collaborations, and career advancements. Mentors offer emotional support and encouragement during challenging times. They serve as a sounding board for ideas and a source of reassurance and motivation.

Reflect on your goals list you created and areas where you need guidance. Define what you hope to achieve with the help of a mentor. Seek potential mentors within your network, industry, or community. Experience, willingness to help, good communication skills, and shared values are crucial qualities to look for in a mentor. If you have an official mentor, be considerate and appreciative of their efforts.

Having a mentor is not just about acquiring knowledge or advancing in your career; it's about transforming your trajectory in life. A mentor can illuminate paths you might not have seen, offer wisdom honed through experience, and provide unwavering support during challenges. The guidance and insight gained from a mentor can propel you toward greater personal growth, professional success, and fulfillment. As you continue on your journey, remember that mentorship is a reciprocal relationship—both parties learn and grow together. Embrace the opportunities that mentorship brings, and let it inspire you to reach new heights and achieve your aspirations with confidence and clarity.

Reflective Exercise:

Seeking a Mentor: Reaching out and finding a mentor can open doors to great advice and growth opportunities.

Instructions:

1. Identify Potential Mentors: Consider individuals in your network or

community who possess qualities you admire or who are accomplished in areas relevant to your goals.
2. Approach Strategy: Plan how you will approach your potential mentor. Consider sending a polite email, scheduling a coffee meeting, or connecting through a mutual acquaintance.
3. Set Mentorship Goals: Write down specific goals you hope to achieve through mentorship. These goals may include acquiring new skills, expanding your professional network, or gaining career advice.
4. Expected Benefits: Reflect on how this mentorship relationship can help you achieve your goals and advance your personal and professional development.

By engaging in this reflective exercise and action step, you actively seek guidance and support from mentors who can inspire and empower you on your journey toward personal growth and achievement. Use these insights to forge meaningful mentorship relationships that can enrich your life and career.

"A mentor is someone who sees more talent and ability within you, than you see in yourself, and helps bring it out of you."
— *Bob Proctor*

Chapter Twelve: The Path to Spiritual Fulfillment

Spiritual fulfillment is a chapter close to my heart. This isn't about converting you to a particular religion or debating the concept of God as you see it. It's about guiding you closer to your soul self, helping you live passionately with a deep sense of peace, calm, purpose, and connection to something greater than ourselves. If you're reading this book, it's likely that you're already on a spiritual journey or about to embark on one.

So, what is a spiritual journey? It's a path that focuses more on emotions and inner growth rather than the physical aspects of life. As we walk this path, we navigate through difficult and often dark areas, striving to understand ourselves at a deeper soul level. It's a journey of healing and self-discovery, where we begin to sense a higher power guiding us. This journey closely resembles Joseph Campbell's Hero's Journey, where an individual embarks on a quest of self-discovery, facing challenges and tests, ultimately emerging as a more evolved and spiritually enriched person.

For many, the spiritual journey begins when they engage in intuitive work and start connecting with this higher power. My journey started when I felt deeply unsatisfied with my life and began searching for something more meaningful. I sought guidance from psychics, which eventually led me to a spiritual church where I discovered my true calling. Through deep reflection, I realized I was a naturally gifted medium and intuitive.

Embracing this path of being a medium and intuitive helped me recognize that life is more than a 60-hour work week that drains your energy. This realization led me to move to Vancouver Island, seeking a life filled with new possibilities and adventures. My journey, as I describe in *Soul Dance*, was far from what I expected. After enduring turmoil, I found peace and contentment along this path, much like Dorothy in *The Wizard of Oz*, who searched for something outside herself, only to discover that it was her own soul she was seeking.

My interpretation of Dorothy's journey mirrors my own: searching through trauma and turmoil only to find my true soul self beneath it all. This healing process has led me to a life filled with promise, peace, and contentment, where I am deeply connected to my soul self. Your journey might look different, but the essence remains the same—seeking, healing, and ultimately finding fulfillment within.

We're all connected to something greater, and we all have the ability to connect with our soul. The journey to spiritual enlightenment begins with knowing ourselves, listening to the whispers of our soul, and creating a peaceful environment. I believe we all have the ability to be intuitive. It is something I am passionate about. I am now writing a book on intuition called *Blossoming Intuition*, to help people develop there intuition.

To me the word spiritual is when you connect to the innermost parts of yourself and feel a presence bigger then just your physical body. That is the connection of you and you soul. It's an inward journey, a personal exploration which I like to refer to as the spiritual journey. It's a voyage of self-discovery and self-realization. This journey is unique to each person. It's a deeply personal and often transformative experience.

During my spiritual journey, I have connected with something greater than myself, which I like to call the Great Spirit. Some people refer to it as the Source, the God of their understanding, or the Universe. What you call it is a personal choice. In this book I also refer to the soul. It took me years of self study to finally try to understand what the soul really is. I write about this in my book *Soul Discovery*, that will be published in 2025.

Each person has a unique soul, by listening to its whispers, you come closer to the Great Spirit and the universe. The soul is eternally yours. Your soul is like your fingerprint, a unique realm within you. It has boundless potential for spiritual insight, and you don't need to look outside yourself for answers. The soul is a vessel for your spirit. While each soul is distinct, it remains connected to the Great Spirit.

Each soul's journey is unique and continues to evolve, expanding into its true God self, much like layers of Russian stacking dolls. The spirit, different from the soul, represents the energy or essence within a person. It serves as a guiding force, leading us back to our origin. The goal of the spirit is to align with our soul's pure purpose, illuminating our path toward spiritual enlightenment.

Each of us has an incredible power within. I believe it's important to trust the power we have inside ourselves. When we truly tap into this inner strength, we can break free from limiting beliefs and connect deeply with the powerful core of who we are—our Higher Self, our Soul.

I believe that by quieting your mind, you can connect with your higher self and hear the whispers of your soul guiding you along your path. This is possible for everyone. For me, this is what finding your faith and the path to spiritual fulfillment is all about. To put it all simply, it is to listen to your gut.

I found my self drawn to spirit when my mother passed away and my world fell apart. She was the only person who believed in me and loved me unconditionally. Her death felt like the loss of that love and belief. However, I found my faith when I discovered spirituality. I discovered that spirituality has no boundaries. It is open for your heart to experience the universe. Each of us has the power to create worlds.

During my grieving process, I began to hear, see, feel, and sense spirit all around me, more strongly than before. I felt my mother's presence, which gave me hope and inspiration that life is eternal. We are energy, and when we pass, we move into the energetic field. This belief may not be for everyone, but it is true for me. I can hear spirits' whispers and was trained as a platform medium, delivering messages from the spirit world to live audiences.

As I planned this book on passionate living with less, I knew I had to include a chapter on faith. Believing in something greater than ourselves can inspire us to greatness. If there is a higher power, as I believe, it can guide and transform us, helping us achieve new ways of thinking and living.

What shaped me spiritually was when I started to channel spirit. I channel what is called "the collective souls", a group of energetic beings that were once living people. They have evolved and now work through me. I am continually working on my abilities as a spiritual medium. Without an official mentor, the process of learning and advancing is slower than I would like, but I believe in the higher power and its magic.

My strong belief in spirit has given me faith that things will be okay. It has helped me live confidently and passionately, embracing life despite the challenges of living in poverty. Faith is not just about religion; it's about believing in something or someone.

When I lost everything due to my brain health issues, I lost faith in the world and in spirituality. I spiraled into a very dark place. However, faith proved to be essential in my recovery. As I started to get better, I regained faith in people and myself. I delved into spiritual studies, which led me to write this book and to inspire others. Faith can lead to personal growth, emotional well-being, and inner peace.

To move from a place of non-faith, dive deep into yourself through journaling and meditation. My friend Amy, for example, found faith through the 12-Step program, particularly step three, which involves turning your life over to a higher power. Amy is not religious; she is spiritual. The 12-Step program is a spiritual program that has profoundly helped her grow. Each of us has our stories of faith. If you take a moment to look within, you will find your higher being and realize that something is there, guiding and helping you.

Finding faith, in whatever form it takes for you, is a deeply personal and transformative journey. It's about connecting with something greater than yourself, whether that is a higher power, the collective energy of the universe, or simply the strength and wisdom within you. Faith provides the foundation for resilience, hope, and passionate living, especially during challenging times. As you continue to explore your spiritual path, remember that faith is not confined by boundaries; it is an ever-evolving source of inspiration and strength. Embrace it with an open heart, and let it guide you towards a life of fulfillment, purpose, and inner peace.

Reflective Exercises:

1: Nature's Wisdom

Purpose: Connect with the serenity of nature to deepen your spiritual reflection and insight.

- Instructions:
    A. Nature Walk: Find a peaceful outdoor setting, such as a park, forest, or beach. Sit in silence, observe your surroundings, and immerse yourself in the natural environment.
    B. Journaling Prompt: Reflect on your experience in nature by journaling about your thoughts, emotions, and any spiritual insights gained.
    C. Spiritual Connection: Explore how spending time in nature enhances your spiritual journey and fosters a deeper connection with your soul.

2: Journaling Your Spiritual Journey

Purpose: Document and explore your unique spiritual path through journaling.

- Instructions:
    - A. Reflective Journaling: Set aside dedicated time to journal about your spiritual journey. Begin by recalling significant milestones, experiences, and beliefs.
    - B. Themes and Lessons: Identify recurring themes or lessons learned throughout your spiritual journey. Reflect on how these insights have shaped your beliefs and practices.
    - C. Personal Growth: Consider how your spiritual journey has contributed to your personal growth, resilience, and understanding of life's deeper meaning.

By engaging in these reflective exercises, connect with nature's wisdom, and document your spiritual journey. Use journaling as a tool for introspection, self-discovery, and for nurturing your spiritual fulfillment.

"The way is not in the sky; the way is in the heart."
– Buddha

Chapter Thirteen: Raising Your Vibration

As an intuitive, empath, and medium, I don't just feel energy—I live and breathe it. It's like having an invisible radar that's always on, scanning the emotional weather of every room, every conversation, and even my own thoughts. I've learned to protect this sensitivity fiercely because it's my compass. And trust me, once you start tuning in to your vibration, you'll never want to lose that awareness. By the end of this book, you'll have your own set of tools to sense when your vibe is sky-high or dragging.

Walking the spiritual path isn't just about meditation and crystals; it's about knowing yourself on a deeper level. For me, it means waking up every day and checking in: How do I feel? Am I radiating the energy I want to put out into the world? Living with less—whether it's fewer possessions, fewer distractions, or fewer toxic relationships—brings clarity. It's a radical form of self-care that keeps me in tune with the universe's subtle whispers, reminding me that I am always supported, even when I don't see it.

The Law of Vibration is like the soundtrack of your life, always playing in the background, setting the mood. Everything around us, from the happiest memories to the heaviest burdens, hums at its own frequency. Ever walked into a room and immediately felt tension so thick you could cut it with a knife? That's vibration at work. And it's not just external; your thoughts, emotions, and even the way you move send out waves that ripple through your life.

Imagine you're a radio station, constantly broadcasting your vibes to the universe. When you're feeling down, it's like tuning into static—nothing flows, and everything feels off. But when you're in your joy, your station is clear, your energy is contagious, and you become a magnet for the good stuff. That's why raising your vibration is a game changer. It's not just woo-woo; it's physics. It's about taking charge of the frequency you emit.

Vibration is everything. It's why I can't channel spirit when I'm having a bad day, why my intuition gets fuzzy when I'm off balance. It's why I've learned to be intentional about how I start my mornings, the people I surround myself with, and the content I consume. If I let my energy slip, it's like trying to drive a car with a misaligned wheel—bumpy, erratic, and likely to crash. When I'm vibrating high, everything clicks into place.

SOULFUL MINIMALISM

Here's the beautiful truth: you are not powerless. You can shift your vibration with a single thought. You can flip the script on a bad day, change the channel on a loop of negative self-talk, and start aligning with the life you actually want. The Law of Attraction isn't just about wishing on a star; it's about meeting the universe halfway. When you show up with a high vibe, you send out a message: I am ready. Ready for the joy, the abundance, the love, and the serendipities that are waiting for me.

So, start tuning in. Notice how you feel around certain people, places, and even your own thoughts. Get curious about your vibes, because raising your vibration is the key to unlocking a life that feels as good on the inside as it looks on the outside. And remember, it's not about being perfect—it's about being present, aware, and committed to showing up as your highest self.

10 Ways to Raise Your Vibration

1. Listen to your favorite music and dance.
2. Do things that make you laugh and smile.
3. Balance your lifestyle.
4. Cultivate Positive Thoughts: Focus on gratitude, affirmations, and positive thinking to shift your mental state.
5. Manage Emotions: Practice emotional awareness and techniques such as deep breathing, meditation, and mindfulness to elevate your mood.
6. Engage in High-Vibration Activities: Surround yourself with uplifting music, nature, art, and other activities that make you feel good.
7. Create a Positive Environment: Declutter your space, bring in elements that make you feel peaceful and happy, and spend time with people who uplift you.
8. Practice Self-Care: Take care of your physical health through diet, exercise, and sufficient rest, as physical well-being significantly impacts your vibration.
9. Positive Thinking: Maintain a positive mindset by focusing on positive people, places and things.
10. Visualization: Use visualization to create a higher vibrational state.

By consistently focusing on these practices, you can raise your vibration, enhance your energy, and live a more fulfilled and joyful life. Remember, the energy you put out into the world comes back to you, so prioritize raising your vibration to attract the life you desire.

Reflective Exercise:

1. Daily Mood Journal:

- At the end of each day, write down how you felt throughout the day. Note specific emotions, thoughts, and events that influenced your mood. After a week, review your entries to see if there are any recurring themes or patterns.

1. Emotional Check-In:

- Set a few moments aside each day to ask yourself: "How am I feeling right now?" Evaluate your emotional state on a scale from 1 (very low) to 10 (very high). Reflect on what might be contributing to your rating.

1. Energy Interaction Journal:

- After each significant interaction (with friends, family, colleagues, etc.), note how you feel. Do certain people raise or lower your vibration? Reflect on these interactions and consider how they impact your overall frequency.

1. Visualization Exercise:

- Close your eyes and visualize yourself surrounded by a light that represents your energy. What color is it? Is it bright or dim? Reflect on what this visualization might indicate about your current vibrational state.

"What you think you become. What you feel you attract. What you imagine you create."

SOULFUL MINIMALISM

–Buddha

Chapter Fourteen: Trusting Your Gut - A Guide to Intuition

We now understand the importance of vibration and how essential it is for creating what we want in the world and maintaining a peaceful life. Now, let's dive into intuition. Intuition and vibration are closely related because they both involve energy. Intuition speaks in vibrations, not words. It's about following your gut, going with the flow, and listening to your heart. These are all vibrational ways we can understand and connect with our intuition.

I feel that my intuitive journey began when I was little. I always had gut feelings, but it wasn't until my mother passed away that I started paying attention to them. Soon after her passing, spirituality found me, grabbed hold of my soul, and pulled me into this wonderful world of intuition.

I began visiting psychics regularly to discover what was in store for me and my life. It was during this time that my good friend Joyce told me about a spiritual church that offered readings and courses. Excitedly, I signed up for both readings and a psychic development course. This course aimed to help participants develop their intuitive abilities and expand them into psychic skills.

I remember the very first class in this program. I felt scared and out of place—what did I know about psychic development or anything related to it? Nevertheless, I joined in. We began with meditation. Having never meditated before, I sheepishly did my best to stay awake and be mindful of the present moment. As we meditated, words started running through my mind. One word was "frog," the next was "compost," and then "organization." I felt embarrassed when the teacher told us to give a message to someone in the classroom. I pointed to a girl who caught my attention, trusting my gut about who I should give a message to. I told her what I received in the meditation: frog, compost, and organization.

To my surprise, she started to laugh. My initial reaction was embarrassment, but then she explained. That very day, she had been googling frogs because they were causing problems in her compost area, and she needed to organize it. I was stunned—she was amazed by what I told her. That was my very first experience dealing with my intuition in a classroom setting.

SOULFUL MINIMALISM

I have always had a strong sense of intuition, and as I grew older, I became more aware of its power. I often know how situations will unfold, and it can be daunting when I don't follow my intuition. It's like feeling a strong pull toward the right decision and ignoring it has led to disastrous outcomes. For instance, when I had my brain health issue and sought help from Harry, my spiritual minister, I sensed our conversation would end poorly—and it did. Since then, I have done my best to follow my intuition daily, moment by moment.

When it comes to my intuition, I can usually sense a person's core emotional state. I can tell if they are sad or happy, and I can read their energy to understand the type of person they are. During a reading, I tune into the person and feel their energy, sensing their life experiences and emotional needs. I can tell if they need healing or if they are centered within themselves, and I can always sense if they are open and receptive to me and my abilities.

My intuition is so strong that I often take it for granted. However, during readings, I am reminded of its power as I pick up on small details about a person's life. Although I don't like to give predictions due to the concept of free will, I have been known to intuitively sense events before they happen, and they usually do. Growing up, I had premonitions of people dying, often through dreams, which would come true days later. This was stressful but something I have become accustomed to.

Intuition is not always about doom and gloom. For example, it is liberating to know whether you are on the right track in life. I have grown used to letting my intuition guide me daily. While there are times when I am tired and fail to follow this guidance, for the most part, I rely on my intuition. For example, I did a reading for my friend Maple and accurately predicted several things, including a new baby in her family. Her nephew's wife soon found out she was pregnant shortly after her nephew had passed away. Getting validation like this brings me joy, knowing that my readings create happiness for those I help.

I am passionate about many things, and developing intuition is one of them. When I first came to the island where I now live, I went on to teach an intuitive class called Intuition 101, back in the day when no one was teaching such topics. Now, that subject is everywhere. I began teaching intuitive development to ordinary people who wanted to learn about intuition. I believe everyone can learn to be intuitive—it is a gift from the universe. I have written a book on intuition called *Blossoming Intuition*, which will soon be available for purchase. I decided to write this book to reach more people worldwide rather than just teach it locally.

Think of intuition as a muscle: the more you flex it, the stronger it grows. Trusting your intuition can be challenging, but how do you nurture this trust? It comes through consistent practice and the undeniable evidence that your inner knowing is an ally, ever present to guide and support you.

In our world, energy is everything, and at your core, you are an energetic being experiencing human life. You receive information energetically before it fully registers in your conscious mind. This can often confuse sensitive and empathic people, making them feel overwhelmed. The good news is, you can learn to control these experiences and use this energy to your advantage!

Intuition is like the silent language of the soul. It guides our choices and decisions with a wisdom beyond logic. This intuitive power is deeply personal and often seen as our link to the divine. It connects our finite lives to the infinite universe, giving us access to knowledge, insight, and spiritual guidance.

By embracing our intuition, we gain a deeper understanding of our place in the cosmos and invite the divine to light our path. In moments of intuitive clarity, we stand at the crossroads of the ordinary and the mystical, feeling connected to something greater than ourselves.

To discover your intuition and unlock your psychic abilities, an open mind is your best friend. You must acknowledge a higher power that surrounds and encompasses you. The journey to self-awareness and realizing your potential begins with an honest look at your current state. This is your path to enlightenment and uncovering your true self.

Defining Intuition:

Intuition is a more general and widely recognized concept that doesn't necessarily involve psychic phenomena. It refers to the ability to understand or know something without the need for conscious reasoning or logical analysis. Intuition often comes in the form of gut feelings, hunches, or instincts. Here are some key aspects of intuition:

1. Inner Knowing: Intuition is often described as a deep inner knowing or a sense of certainty about a situation or decision, even when there is no apparent logical basis for it.

2. Fast Processing: Intuition can operate quickly, allowing you to make split-second decisions or judgments based on subconscious information and patterns.

3. Emotional Guidance: Intuition can be closely linked to emotions. You may feel drawn toward something or someone because of a positive intuitive feeling or, conversely, feel uneasy due to a negative intuitive sense.

4. Enhanced Perception: Developing your intuition can lead to heightened perception of subtle cues, body language, and non-verbal communication.

5. Problem Solving: Many people use intuition as a problem-solving tool, relying on their inner guidance to help them navigate challenges or make choices.

Defining an Empath:

Empaths are individuals with heightened sensitivity who thrive in the realm of intuition and emotions. They often possess a strong artistic inclination and a remarkable attunement to the energies that envelop them. These highly sensitive individuals can easily become emotionally overwhelmed due to their ability to absorb excessive energies. Empaths may struggle with certain television shows, movies, and programs, and particular sounds or crowded spaces can disturb them. Their emotional state can be significantly influenced by their surroundings, either burdening or uplifting them. Empaths possess an exceptional receptivity that enables them to connect with people on a profound level.

Defining Psychic Abilities:

I'm a firm believer that everyone has the potential to unlock their psychic abilities—it's not just a gift reserved for a select few. Think of it as your secret superpower, hidden within, waiting to be discovered. These abilities, often called the sixth sense, are about tuning into a deeper layer of reality that goes beyond what our eyes see, ears hear, or hands touch. Psychic abilities aren't some mysterious magic; they're a natural part of who we are, rooted in our inner selves. The trick is learning how to tap into this wild, wondrous aspect of ourselves.

You've probably heard people lump psychic abilities and intuition together, but let's clear that up. While they're like cousins, they're not identical twins. Intuition is that gut feeling, the little nudge that tells you to trust or steer clear, while psychic abilities take things up a notch with experiences that can feel downright supernatural—think visions, messages, or premonitions. Intuition is a broader, everyday sense that anyone can cultivate, whereas psychic abilities often involve more specific, sometimes paranormal, encounters. But here's the cool part: both can be nurtured and developed, enriching how you connect with the world and yourself.

And no, psychics aren't mind readers, despite what you might see in movies. They don't have a crystal ball with all your secrets tucked inside. What they do have is a sensitivity to energy—your energy. This isn't just about seeing ghosts or predicting the future; it's about picking up on the vibes that surround you, tapping into the layers of your subconscious, your aura, and your heart. Some psychics are deeply attuned to the material world and others might venture into the spiritual, but it's not a one-size-fits-all ability. Think of them as "sensitives," people whose connection to their inner world often heightens their psychic experiences. So, if you're feeling a pull toward exploring your own abilities, trust it. You might just be a little more sensitive than you thought.

Benefits of Developing Intuition

- Improved decision-making
- Enhanced creativity
- Better alignment with life's purpose
- Increased self-awareness
- Reduced stress levels
- More confidence
- Better problem-solving
- More faith
- More trust

Techniques to Enhance Intuition

1. Mindfulness and Meditation

    - Practicing mindfulness to quiet the mind. By focusing on the present moment and letting go of distractions, you create a mental space where your intuition can flourish.
    - Guided meditations for intuition

SOULFUL MINIMALISM

1. Journaling

- Keeping an intuition journal
- Reflecting on intuitive insights and experiences

1. Trusting Your Gut

- Engage in activities that stimulate your creativity, such as drawing, painting, or playing music. This activities can help you access a more intuitive state of mind and strengthen your gut feelings.
- Learn to differentiate between intuition and fear

1. Listening to Your Body

- Pay close attention to your body's signals. When faced with a decision, tune into how your body feels. Does your stomach tighten or relax? Do you feel a sense of ease or discomfort? Your body often gives you clues about the right course of action. It is important to understand your physical cues and signals.

1. Connecting with Nature

- Grounding techniques: take your shoes off and walk on the grass.
- Spend time in nature, away from the distractions of daily life. Walking in nature can help you connect with your inner self and heighten your intuitive awareness.

How Intuitive are you? Quiz

Instructions:

For each question, choose the response that best describes your experiences and tendencies. Be honest with yourself, as this quiz is designed to help you better understand your intuitive abilities.

1. When faced with an important decision, I tend to: a) Rely on logical analysis and pros and cons lists. b) Follow my initial gut feeling without overthinking it. c) Seek advice from others before making a choice.

2. Have you ever experienced a "gut feeling" or strong intuition that later proved to be accurate? a) Rarely or never. b) Occasionally, but not consistently. c) Frequently, and it has been accurate.

3. How often do you recall having vivid dreams that seemed to contain symbolic or meaningful messages? a) Rarely or never. b) Occasionally, but not often. c) Frequently, and I often find meaning in my dreams.

4. In social situations, I am more likely to: a) Focus on facts and external cues. b) Tune into the emotions and energies of others. c) Balance both logic and intuition in my interactions.

5. When meeting someone new, I often: a) Form judgments based on appearance and behavior. b) Get a sense of their personality and emotions quickly. c) Take my time to get to know them before forming an opinion.

6. How do you react when faced with unexpected challenges or crises? a) Feel overwhelmed and uncertain. b) Trust my instincts to guide me through the situation. c) Seek advice and gather information before deciding on a course of action.

7. Have you ever had a premonition or a sense of something about to happen before it occurred? a) Never. b) Once or twice, but it's rare. c) Yes, multiple times, and some were significant events.

8. In your daily life, do you often experience déjà vu or a sense of familiarity with new places or people? a) Rarely or never. b) Occasionally, but not frequently. c) Frequently, and it can feel quite uncanny.

Scoring:

- Give yourself 1 point for each (a) response.
- Give yourself 2 points for each (b) response.
- Give yourself 3 points for each (c) response.

Interpretation:

- 8-12 points: You have some intuitive tendencies, but you may benefit from further exploring and developing your intuition.
- 13-18 points: You have moderate intuitive abilities and may experience intuitive insights from time to time.
- 19-24 points: You possess strong intuitive capabilities and are likely in

SOULFUL MINIMALISM

tune with your inner guidance.

Reflective Exercises
1. Intuitive Journaling
Materials Needed: Journal, pen, quiet space.

- Find a quiet space where no one will disturb you.
- Close your eyes, take a few deep breaths, and focus on your breathing for a couple of minutes.
- Ask yourself a specific question or focus on a topic you'd like guidance on.
- Open your eyes and start writing without overthinking. Let your hand move freely, writing whatever comes to mind.
- After 10-15 minutes, read what you've written. Reflect on any insights or patterns that emerge.

2. Intuitive Drawing
Materials Needed: Paper, colored pencils, or markers.

- Sit quietly and close your eyes. Take deep breaths to center yourself.
- Imagine you are drawing your current feelings or a question you have.
- Open your eyes and start drawing whatever comes to mind. Don't worry about making it look perfect; focus on expressing your feelings or thoughts through colors and shapes.
- Once finished, look at your drawing and reflect on what it represents. Write down any thoughts or feelings that arise.

3. Meditation with Intuitive Visualization
Materials Needed: Comfortable place to sit or lie down, calming music (optional).

- Find a comfortable position and close your eyes. Take deep breaths to relax your mind, body and soul.
- Visualize a peaceful place where you feel completely at ease.
- In this place, imagine meeting a wise guide or mentor. Ask this guide

a question you've been pondering.
- Listen carefully to any messages or feelings that come to you.
- After the meditation, write down your experience and any insights you received.

4. Daily Intuitive Check-In
Materials Needed: Journal or a piece of paper, pen.

- Every morning or evening, take a few minutes to check in with your intuition.
- Sit quietly and take a few deep breaths.
- Ask yourself, "What do I need to know today."
- Write down whatever comes to mind, even if it doesn't make immediate sense.
- Reflect on these notes at the end of the week and see if any patterns or insights emerge.

5. Dream Analysis
Materials Needed: Dream journal, pen.

- Keep a journal by your bed and write down the dreams immediately, as soon as your rise so you don't forget them. Consider my dream journal called *Moonlit Insights* available on amazon.
- Review your dream journal weekly, looking for recurring symbols, themes, or messages.
- Reflect on how these dreams might be connected to your intuition and current life situations.

6. The Guessing Game
This exercise is designed to help you develop and strengthen your intuition by practicing prediction and reflection.

Materials Needed: Journal, pen.

Before the Event:

SOULFUL MINIMALISM

- Choose an Event: Select an upcoming event, outing, or engagement you will be attending. This could be a social gathering, a meeting, a dinner party, or even a casual outing with friends.
- Quiet Reflection: Find a quiet space where you can sit undisturbed for a few minutes. Close your eyes, take a few deep breaths, and center yourself.
- Visualize the Event: In your mind's eye, visualize the event in detail. Imagine arriving, interacting with others, and any activities that might take place. Pay attention to any feelings, images, or thoughts that come to you during this visualization.
- Intuitive Guess: After a few minutes, open your eyes and write down your intuitive guesses about how the event will unfold. Include details such as:
    1. Who you might meet or interact with.
    2. The overall mood or atmosphere of the event.
    3. Any significant conversations or occurrences.
    4. Any feelings or impressions you have about the event.

During the Event:

- Stay Present: As you attend the event, stay present and mindful. Observe your surroundings, interactions, and the flow of the event.
- Note Any Intuitive Hits: Pay attention to any moments where you feel a sense of déjà vu or recognition from your earlier visualization. Mentally note these instances.

After the Event:

- Reflect and Compare: Once the event is over, find a quiet space again and reflect on your experience. Take out your journal and compare your intuitive guesses with what actually happened. Write down:
    - What aspects of your prediction were accurate.
    - Any surprises or unexpected occurrences.
    - How closely your intuition matched the reality of the event.
- Analyze Your Intuition: Reflect on how you felt during the intuitive

guessing phase and during the event. Were there any strong intuitive hits? Did any specific feelings or images come true?

Regular Practice:

- Repeat the Exercise: Practice this exercise regularly with different types of events. The more you practice, the more you will tune into your intuitive abilities.
- Track Your Progress: Keep a dedicated section in your journal to track your progress. Note any patterns or improvements in your intuitive accuracy over time.

By engaging in The Guessing Game, you will become more attuned to your intuitive insights and will develop greater confidence in your ability to predict and navigate future events.

"The only real valuable thing is intuition."
—Albert Einstein

Chapter Fifteen: Gratitude and Appreciation

I remember when I first took my spiritual healing course. One of the exercises was called Gratefulness and Appreciation. You were to pick a partner and, without the partner talking or commenting, tell them what you are grateful and appreciative for—for five entire minutes. It sounds easy enough. However, at that time, I had just lost my mother, father, my two dogs who were like my children, gone through a divorce, and lost one of my good friends. I felt like I had nothing. Nothing to give back, nothing to be grateful for.

I started to fill up with anxiety and panic. I burst into tears, ran out of the class, and went to the bathroom to collect myself. I did my best to recover my ego and pride and continued the exercise with my partner. I will never forget that moment. It was a horrific time for me, not being able to find anything to be appreciative or grateful for. Back then, I had 16 beauty salons and was in the process of expanding my beauty empire and starting a charity for impoverished seniors to get their hair done for free so they could feel special. But none of that mattered at the time; I was not in the space to be grateful or appreciative.

I continued with the course and soon after, I experienced a manic episode and went into psychosis, which led to my *Soul Dance* journey. After that, it became even harder to be grateful and appreciative because I lost everything—my beauty empire, my belongings, and I thought, my soul.

In one of my intuition classes, I would do the Appreciation and Gratitude exercise. I did it with the class, thinking I was brave to do so. No one, however, knew how brave I was because they did not know the story of the day I ran out of my healing class. As I did the exercise with the students, I started to swell up with anxiety and have a panic attack. I did my best to control it with deep breathing so the students wouldn't notice, but my voice betrayed me. One student jokingly commented on it, and I brushed it off.

Back then, I was closed off, unable to show my true colors and heart to anyone because of all the loss that had occurred. It was an excruciatingly difficult time. You may be asking, how did I find my groove again? By following all the steps in this book, *Soulful Minimalism*. Little by little, I started to get my groove back and began to dance under the moonlight with my soul.

It took me almost 10 years to regain my stride after my mother passed and everything fell apart. It was an excruciating time for me, but after years of self-development, I finally started to see the light again. I began to heal. I followed the processes in this book, and they worked for me. Back then, I wasn't aware that these were processes. All I knew was that they were feeding my soul. So I dived deeper into what felt good and made me happy.

When I started working part-time at the local hair shop to supplement my income, I would use my earnings to purchase courses. That's where my money went—to better myself, and it felt right. I kept working hard on self-development any moment I got. Then COVID hit, and I lost my job for a while. During that time, I engrossed myself in education, studying during every waking moment. This led me to my passion: recreating myself. This journey made me more appreciative and grateful for what I have.

I wasn't fully aware of the significance of the healing that had begun, but I was starting to heal. It wasn't until I moved to this tranquil paradise in the country, where I have an extra space for my writing, that I started to realize how grateful and appreciative I am today.

Appreciation isn't just a polite "thank you"; it's a full-hearted embrace of everything in your life, big and small. It's about noticing the sparkle in the mundane, the magic in the moments we often overlook. To truly attract what we desire, we've got to fall in love with our lives—all of it. When we make appreciation a daily habit, it becomes a powerful game changer, a secret sauce for manifesting abundance. It's like tuning into a higher frequency radio station where opportunities, joy, and unexpected blessings are constantly playing your favorite songs.

When you start vibing on appreciation, something incredible happens: those low-frequency moments—where you feel stuck, down, or settling for less—start to fade into the background. Suddenly, you're not just surviving; you're thriving. You're drawn toward things that lift you up, and life begins to mirror that energy back to you. Appreciation isn't just about attracting more of what you want; it's about shifting your entire perspective, zooming in on what's working instead of what's not, and letting gratitude guide the way.

Now, let's get clear on the difference between gratitude and appreciation, because they're not quite the same. Think of gratitude as the feeling you get after a storm—you've made it through, and you're thankful for the lessons learned. It's beautiful, but it often carries the weight of the struggle you overcame. Appreciation, on the other hand, is pure, unfiltered love. It's like basking in the sunlight on a perfect day with no hint of a cloud in sight. It's being fully in the moment, without the baggage of past hardships. Appreciation aligns us directly with source energy, amplifying our vibration and putting us in the sweet spot to receive more of what lights us up.

Appreciation is not just about recognizing the positive aspects of our lives; it's about fully immersing ourselves in those moments and letting that positive energy elevate us. Here's how we can expand on this concept:

1. Daily Practice of Appreciation

- Start each day by listing three things you appreciate about your life. This could be anything from a supportive friend to the beauty of nature around you. This simple practice sets a positive tone for the day and aligns your vibration with abundance.

1. Mindful Moments

- Throughout your day, take mindful moments to pause and appreciate your surroundings. Whether it's a brief moment of silence or a deep breath of fresh air, these pauses can help you stay connected to the high-frequency energy of appreciation.

1. Expressing Appreciation to Others

- Make it a habit to express your appreciation to others. A simple thank you or a heartfelt compliment can not only uplift the recipient but also amplify your own sense of gratitude and connection.

1. Transformative Power of Appreciation

- Recognize that appreciation can transform challenging situations. By finding something to appreciate even in difficult times, you shift your focus from what's wrong to what's right, creating a positive shift in your energy and perspective.

While gratitude is a powerful emotion that often follows the resolution of challenges, appreciation takes this a step further by allowing us to connect directly with the positive energies of the universe. When we move from gratitude to appreciation, we shift from a reactive state to a proactive one, where our focus is on the continuous flow of positive energy.

Appreciation is a higher vibrational state that aligns us with source energy, enhancing our ability to manifest our desires. By practicing appreciation, we not only attract more of what we want but also create a ripple effect that brings more joy, love, and abundance into our lives and the lives of those around us.

Embrace the practice of appreciation and let it become a cornerstone of your journey towards living passionately with less. Through the power of appreciation, you can transform your life, elevate your vibration, and unlock the abundance that awaits you.

Reflective Exercise:

1. Appreciation & Gratitude Journal:

- Keep a journal where you regularly write about things you appreciate and are grateful for. This can include people, experiences, personal achievements, or even simple pleasures. Reflecting on these entries can help reinforce the habit of appreciation and keep your focus on positive aspects. Consider my Appreciation and Gratitude journal called *Seeds of Thanks- Gratitude and Appreciation Journal*, available on amazon.
- At the end of each day, set aside time to reflect on both your gratitudes and appreciations. Write down at least three things you are grateful for and three things you appreciate, along with the reasons for each.

2. Gratitude Letter:

- Choose someone in your life for whom you are particularly grateful. Write a heartfelt letter or note expressing your gratitude, detailing specific reasons and examples of why you are grateful for them.
- Reflect on how expressing your gratitude to others affects your

relationship with them and your own emotional state. Consider:
- How did the person respond to your expression of gratitude?
- How did expressing gratitude make you feel?

By consistently engaging in these reflective exercises, you will have a heightened sense of both gratitude and appreciation. This practice will strengthen your connection to positive vibrations and the abundant energy of the universe, enhancing your overall well-being and enriching your spiritual journey.

"Gratitude turns what we have into enough."
– Anonymous

Chapter Sixteen: Nourishment From the Inside Out

When it comes to nourishing my mind, it's easy. I constantly feed it by studying and learning. However, nourishing my body is more challenging due to financial restrictions. When I had my beauty empire, I could afford organic foods, regular massages, spa treatments, and visits to a naturopathic doctor. I could buy any vitamins and supplements I needed and even had a personal trainer to help me stay fit. Nourishing the physical body is easy when you have money. But when you're living with financial constraints, it proves to be much more challenging.

Taking care of your physical body is essential, especially on a tight budget. Nourishing your body, mind, and soul might seem challenging when resources are limited, and it can be easy to neglect self-care when facing financial constraints or battling depression. However, prioritizing your well-being is vital for leading a fulfilling life. By making mindful choices and cultivating a positive mindset, you can enhance your overall health and happiness without breaking the bank.

I know it can be difficult to take care of yourself from the inside out. I know this because it is one of the challenges in my life. Living with bipolar disorder is a struggle for me. While I strive to maintain a balanced life, when things go wrong, my vibration plummets to the ground, and it hits me harder than it would if I didn't have a mental disorder. When this happens, self-care becomes challenging, to say the least. That is my hardcore reality.

Another issue with not being able to nourish myself properly, particularly with healthy food, is that I simply cannot afford it. I rely on the food bank twice a month, which helps me out greatly, but a lot of the food available is processed. This makes it challenging to nourish myself from the inside out. So, what do I do to help myself with this trouble of not being able to nourish myself properly? I do my best, make it a priority, and each day gets better.

For example, I buy apples from Costco because they last longer than most fruit and provide me with essential vitamins. As the saying goes, "An apple a day keeps the doctor away." There is a farmer's market with fresh produce that I try to get to in the summer months, offering affordable fruits and veggies. I also buy a multivitamin for women from Costco; it is an inexpensive way to get all the necessary vitamins when you are on a budget. When I had a bit of extra money, I would buy a vegetable substitute—a liquid form of various vegetables, much like a vitamin. I would purchase this from the health food store to help me get the nourishment I needed from not eating enough vegetables.

If you can, eat healthy organic foods that are non-processed. The best way to go about this is to shop the edges of the grocery store, where most fresh food is located. Small, consistent choices like this can make a significant difference.

Nourishing yourself from the inside out goes beyond just food. It's about creating a holistic approach to well-being that includes mental, emotional, and physical health. Here are some practical strategies to help you nurture yourself holistically, even on a tight budget:

Eating an apple a day offers several health benefits:

1. **Nutrient Rich:** Apples are packed with essential nutrients such as dietary fiber, vitamin C, potassium, and various antioxidants. These nutrients support overall health and well-being.
2. **Digestive Health:** The fiber content in apples, particularly soluble fiber like pectin, helps support healthy digestion by promoting regular bowel movements and feeding beneficial gut bacteria.
3. **Heart Health:** Studies suggest that regular apple consumption may help lower levels of bad cholesterol and reduce the risk of heart disease. The antioxidants in apples, such as flavonoids and polyphenols, contribute to these heart-protective effects.
4. **Weight Management:** Apples are low in calories but high in fiber, making them a satisfying snack choice that can help control appetite and contribute to weight management goals.
5. **Blood Sugar Regulation:** The fiber and polyphenol content in apples can help regulate blood sugar levels, potentially reducing the risk of type 2 diabetes and managing existing conditions.
6. **Hydration:** Apples are naturally hydrating due to their high-water content, aiding in overall hydration when consumed regularly.
7. **Dental Health:** Chewing apples stimulates saliva production, which helps reduce tooth decay by neutralizing acids and washing away food particles.

8. **Antioxidant Properties:** Apples contain antioxidants that protect cells from oxidative stress and inflammation, contributing to overall cellular health and potentially reducing the risk of chronic diseases.

Incorporating an apple into your daily diet can contribute to these health benefits, supporting your overall well-being and providing a delicious and convenient snack option.

Another critical aspect of nourishment is self-love, which nourishes the mental and emotional parts of your being. Practicing self-love involves treating yourself with kindness, respect, and compassion. It also means recognizing your worth and taking time to care for your own needs. This can include setting healthy boundaries, engaging in activities that bring you joy, and speaking kindly to yourself.

For me, overall nourishment has been the most challenging, both physically and emotionally. After completing *Soul Dance*, I was very hard on myself. I did not give myself the love and appreciation I deserved. Through self-reflection and journaling, I discovered that I was very angry with myself for losing everything—very angry. It took over seven years for me to learn that I needed to forgive myself for all the trauma and turmoil I went through.

For years, I did not practice good self-care, both physically and emotionally. I would torture my body by feeding it junk food and alcohol. I would tell myself that I was unworthy, and I reflected that out into the world. This left me as a quiet, reserved person who appeared stuck-up. That couldn't be further from the truth. While I appeared to be uninterested in engaging with people, inside I was frightened and sad—so sad that I felt like breaking down and crying at any given moment when I was in public.

It took a very long time to get over that. Although I may still appear reserved and standoffish, I am actually a fun-loving, happy-go-lucky, easygoing person. Once you get to know me, you will find that I am very loving. However, because of the trauma I endured, I do not showcase the real me to the world. It has taken a lot of self-reflection and self-love to get me on this road to recovery.

I share all this with you because nourishment is so very important. It encompasses more than just the food we eat; it includes how we treat ourselves and the thoughts we entertain. I hope that by sharing my story, you can start to understand yourself on a deeper level and find ways to nourish your body, mind, and soul.

By embracing self-love, practicing forgiveness, and making mindful choices, we can begin to heal and flourish. Nourishment is about creating a holistic approach to well-being that nurtures every aspect of our being. Remember that small, consistent efforts can lead to significant change. Let's make a commitment to nourish ourselves inside and out, fostering a life of health, happiness, and fulfillment.

Reflective Exercise:

1. Develop a Breath Work Routine:

- Engage in deep breathing exercises to alleviate stress and support your digestive system. This practice nourishes both the body and the mind, promoting overall well-being and mental clarity.

1. Dance and Laugh Everyday:

- Find something that makes you laugh and do that everyday
- In the morning while getting ready for your day, put on your favorite tunes and dance.

1. Get into a Routine:

- Get up at the same time everyday
- Do self care routines at the same time daily
- Take vitamins and any medications at the same time everyday

1. Balanced Nutrition on a Budget:

- Prioritize buying fresh, in-season produce when possible.
- Look for budget-friendly sources of protein, such as beans, lentils, and eggs.

1. Mindful Eating:

- Practice eating slowly and savoring each bite to improve digestion and enjoyment.
- Focus on portion control to ensure you're getting the right nutrients without overeating.

1. Emotional Well-being:

- Engage in activities that bring you joy and relaxation, such as reading, listening to music, or spending time in nature.
- Practice gratitude by keeping a journal of things you're thankful for each day.

1. Mental Health:

- Utilize free or low-cost mental health resources, such as community centers, support groups, and online platforms.

1. Physical Activity:

- Find budget-friendly ways to stay active, like walking, yoga, or home workouts.
- Set achievable fitness goals to keep yourself motivated and consistent.

1. Rest and Sleep:

- Establish a regular sleep schedule to improve the quality of your rest.
- Create a calming bedtime routine to help you wind down and prepare for sleep.

1. Hydration:

- Drink plenty of water throughout the day to keep your body hydrated and functioning well.
- Opt for herbal teas or infused water as budget-friendly alternatives to sugary drinks.

SOULFUL MINIMALISM

By implementing these strategies, you can take meaningful steps toward nourishing yourself from the inside out.

"Let food be thy medicine and medicine be thy food."
– Hippocrates

Chapter Seventeen: Living with Compassion

I am an empath and a very compassionate person. Over the years, I have done my best to help people whenever possible; it is simply how I am built. I look around me and see so many compassionate people. Our local town is very caring, with a center for the homeless that provides a safe injection site for those struggling with addiction. When I see these individuals walking around town with little to show for their lives, I wonder what happened to bring them to such a low point. Most likely, trauma and mental illness—depression, bipolar disorder, schizophrenia, or other brain health issues—played a role. Regardless of the cause, it is a difficult road. I know this because I was once on the brink of being homelessness on the street. I often think that if the medication I was given hadn't worked as intended, I could have ended up on the streets just like them. It was compassionate people who helped me along my journey and kept me from ending up on the streets.

Linda is one of the most compassionate individuals I've ever met. I was first introduced to her by my friend Vivienne, who suggested I sign up for a nutrition program. Unbeknownst to Vivienne, I already knew Linda from the rooming house where I lived. When Vivienne told Linda my story, Linda immediately gave me $700 without hesitation, no questions asked. She also offered me a place to stay at her home if I ever needed it, showing incredible generosity and compassion.

Linda's kindness was a lifeline for me during a difficult time. The people in my life now are humble, grateful, and appreciative of everything they have. Each has their unique way of giving back. Amy, for instance, is in a 12-step program that helped heal her life, and she now sponsors others with her whole heart. Fred, a lovely man, volunteers at the local food bank and brings me food when needed. His acts of kindness reflect his compassion and commitment to contributing to society.

Compassionate gestures don't need to be grand. Sometimes, the smallest smile or compliment can make a significant difference in someone's life. You never know what someone might be going through, and a bit of love and kindness can go much further than you think.

SOULFUL MINIMALISM

Compassion isn't just a warm fuzzy feeling—it's a force that can shift your inner world and ripple out to change the world around you. It's that gut-wrenching pull when you see someone struggling, paired with an unwavering urge to make things better. When you live passionately with less, compassion becomes a non-negotiable. It deepens your spiritual journey, sharpens your empathy, and creates a profound connection with others. Opening your heart to the experiences of those around you doesn't just make you a better person; it fills your own life with a richer sense of purpose. In this chapter, we're diving into why compassion matters, how to cultivate it, and how it supercharges your spiritual growth and well-being.

Compassion is more than a passing feeling of sympathy or a tear shed for someone else's pain. It's an active, loving commitment to be present, to show up, and to extend a hand when someone else is in the trenches. It's recognizing our shared human journey, the messy and beautiful truth that we're all in this together. No matter your background or beliefs, compassion is a common thread across every spiritual tradition, emphasizing the power of loving-kindness and selflessness to transform us from the inside out.

When you grow in compassion, you crack open the door to a deeper kind of transformation. It softens the ego, dissolves the "me-first" mentality, and invites a sense of unity with all beings. Compassion challenges us to look beyond our daily gripes and connect to something bigger than ourselves. And this shift in perspective? It's like unlocking a hidden level in the game of life—a deeper understanding of who we are and our place in the universe. When you live with compassion, you're not just ticking boxes or doing good deeds; you're creating a sense of fulfillment that money or accolades can't touch. It's the joy that comes from knowing you've made a difference, however small, in someone else's world.

Compassion and empathy are like dance partners, each moving in rhythm with the other. While empathy lets us feel another person's emotions, compassion is the drive to take that next step—to do something about it. It's empathy in action. And the more we practice compassion, the more finely tuned our empathy becomes. We start to connect with people on a soul level, seeing beyond surface struggles to the shared humanity underneath. It's the glue that binds us closer, fostering relationships that are not just surface-deep but truly meaningful.

Let's face it: human connection is essential. It's what lifts us up, gives us purpose, and makes life worth living. Compassion strengthens these bonds by creating an atmosphere of kindness, patience, and acceptance. When you approach others with a compassionate heart, you're not just helping them; you're building a bridge of trust and mutual respect. It's the kind of connection that can turn strangers into friends and communities into tight-knit families.

Compassion is contagious. A single act of kindness can spark a ripple effect, bringing light to many lives. When we show up for each other, it inspires others to do the same, creating a cycle of positivity that elevates everyone involved. Imagine a world where compassion is the norm—where people feel seen, valued, and supported. That's the power of compassion. It's a quiet revolution that can lead to massive change, promoting peace, cooperation, and a sense of global unity. Compassion isn't just about feeling good; it's about doing good and making the world a little kinder, one act at a time.

And let's not forget—compassion isn't just great for others; it's good for you too. When we act compassionately, our brains release oxytocin, the "love hormone" that makes us feel warm, connected, and calm. It lowers our stress, boosts our mood, and even fires up the brain's reward center, flooding us with feel-good chemicals like dopamine and endorphins. Simply put, compassion makes us happier, healthier, and more at peace. It's a natural antidote to anxiety and self-absorption, pulling our focus away from our own worries and toward the joy of helping others.

Compassion is the cornerstone of strong, lasting relationships. It's the secret sauce that builds trust, loyalty, and deep connections. Acts of kindness lay the foundation for mutual respect and understanding, the building blocks of any healthy relationship. And it doesn't stop at personal bonds—compassion weaves a tighter social fabric, creating communities where people feel valued and supported. By nurturing a culture of compassion, we're not just improving our own lives; we're paving the way for a more inclusive, harmonious world where everyone has each other's backs.

Reflective Exercises

1. Communicate with Kindness

SOULFUL MINIMALISM

Choose your words carefully, ensuring they are gentle and respectful. A kind word can lift someone's spirit and make a significant difference in their day.

1. Apologize Sincerely When You've Made a Mistake

Acknowledge your errors and offer a heartfelt apology. This shows humility and respect for the other person's feelings, paving the way for healing and reconciliation.

1. Listen Attentively and Without Judgment

Practice active listening by fully focusing on the speaker, withholding judgment, and showing empathy. This fosters deeper understanding and connection.

1. Encourage and Support Others

Offer words of encouragement and positive reinforcement. Celebrate others' efforts and achievements, motivating them to keep striving for their goals.

1. Offer Assistance to Someone in Need

Extend a helping hand to those who might be struggling with a task. Your support can alleviate their burden and demonstrate genuine care and compassion.

1. Celebrate the Success of Others

Share in the joy of others' accomplishments. Recognize and applaud their achievements without envy, which strengthens your bond and promotes positivity.

1. Embrace and Accept People as They Are

Practice unconditional acceptance of others, acknowledging their unique qualities and differences. This fosters a more inclusive and compassionate environment.

By engaging in these reflective exercises and daily practices, you can deepen your understanding of compassion and integrate it more fully into your life. This, in turn, will enhance your emotional well-being, strengthen your relationships, and contribute to a more compassionate and connected community.

"If you want others to be happy, practice compassion. If you want to be happy, practice compassion."
– Dalai Lama

Chapter Eighteen: Soulful Service

When I began writing this chapter, I initially felt that I hadn't contributed much to society or to the world. My feelings of inadequacy stemmed from the financial assistance I receive, such as government disability benefits and support from the food bank. Friends often help me with transportation, and I felt reliant on others. However, when I truly reflected on how I have contributed, a different story emerged.

Throughout my life, I've always strived to help others whenever I could. As I grew older, my contributions became more formalized. I volunteered at a local shelter, cutting hair for the homeless, and offered workshops at women's shelters on how to present themselves in a professional environment. These workshops included lessons on hair, makeup, and wardrobe, providing these women with the confidence and skills to re-enter the workforce.

After moving to the island, I founded a charity called Pandora's Box, aimed at helping trauma survivors not just cope, but thrive. This project was a labor of love, inspired by my own experiences with physical abuse and emotional struggle. I reached out to local businesses and rallied 18 contributors, including life coaches, fitness trainers, hairstylists, makeup artists, estheticians, photographers, counselors, and financial advisors. Our mission was to provide comprehensive support to those in need, enabling them to rebuild their lives and flourish.

Candidates would share their traumatic story and, over the course of a year, transform their lives with the help of our contributors. Pandora's Box was my way of giving back to the community and, hopefully, the world. Unfortunately, the project lasted less than three months before I experienced a manic episode that led to psychosis, causing me to lose everything, including the charity. Just before I lost my entire beauty business, I was set to launch the White Light Foundation, a charity dedicated to providing low-income seniors with access to hair services at little to no cost. Sadly, this, too, was lost due to my brain health issues.

Despite this setback, my passion for helping others never waned. During a manic episode, I envisioned a global charity called PurFound, which would involve renovating apartment buildings to create self-sustaining communities.

These communities would feature food gardens, communal kitchens, cafeterias, and laundry services, all provided for free. Residents, who would be people living in poverty, would volunteer their time to maintain these services, fostering a sense of community and mutual support.

Though this grand vision and developed business plan was interrupted by my hospitalization and the subsequent halt of my wild ideas, I never lost hope entirely. It took time, but I regained my faith and passion for life. Now, I contribute by volunteering at a local art exhibition annually, which is my way of giving back at this stage of my recovery.

I still dream of reviving Pandora's Box, making it bigger and better than before, and perhaps even realizing PurFound one day. These dreams fuel my desire to help others and remind me that, despite the challenges, we all have the potential to contribute meaningfully to the world.

Contribution is like a hidden key to unlocking deeper spiritual growth and personal fulfillment. It's not just about giving what you have; it's about showing up with what you are—your time, your skills, your love, and your compassion. Whether it's lending a helping hand, sharing a kind word, or simply being present for someone, contributing to the world around you is one of the most soul-satisfying things you can do. It's not about grand gestures or big bank accounts; it's about the small, everyday acts of kindness that remind us we're all in this together.

When you step outside of yourself to help someone else, you feel a rush of purpose that money can't buy. Suddenly, life's not just about the daily grind or material gains; it's about those soul-nourishing moments that fill your heart and light you up from the inside.

Giving also helps us see the bigger picture, creating a sense of connection and unity that goes way beyond our individual concerns. You're no longer just one person navigating life's ups and downs—you're part of a larger, interconnected human family. Acts of contribution align you with the higher principles of love, kindness, and service, turning every small gesture into a step toward deeper spiritual understanding and personal growth.

So, how does giving tie into living a passionate life with less? Simple: it's all about shifting your focus from what you don't have to what you can offer. Living passionately on less means seeing the richness of life in moments, relationships, and experiences rather than things. Contribution flips the script from scarcity to abundance because every time you give, you realize how much you actually have to offer. It cultivates gratitude, sparks resilience, and pushes you to be creative in ways you never thought possible.

Giving also has a sneaky way of revealing hidden strengths and talents you didn't even know you had. Maybe you find joy in mentoring someone, discover a knack for organizing community events, or simply realize how much your words can lift someone's day. These moments are like little breadcrumbs leading you to new avenues for personal growth and self-expression. It's in these acts of contribution that you find yourself, not by accumulating more stuff, but by giving away what truly matters.

Living a life rooted in purposeful contribution is about crafting a life filled with passion, connection, and alignment with your deepest values. It's proof that you don't need a lot to live richly—you just need to give from the heart. By embracing contribution, you turn every day into an opportunity to connect, grow, and make a difference, both in your world and within yourself.

Benefits of Soulful Service:

1. Enhanced Sense of Purpose and Fulfillment:

- Personal Growth: Contributing to the well-being of others and the community fosters a deep sense of purpose and meaning in life. It allows individuals to connect with something larger than themselves, promoting personal growth and self-discovery.
- Fulfillment: Knowing that one's actions positively impact others brings a profound sense of fulfillment and satisfaction. This emotional reward enhances overall well-being and happiness.

1. Strengthened Connections and Relationships:

- Building Community: Contribution often involves collaborating with others toward a common goal, whether through volunteering, activism, or supporting local causes. This fosters bonds with like-minded individuals and strengthens community ties.
- Enhanced Social Support: Engaging in acts of contribution can expand social networks and create supportive relationships.

1. Promotion of Personal Well-Being:

- Reduced Stress and Anxiety: Acts of kindness and service have been shown to reduce stress levels and alleviate symptoms of anxiety. Contributing to others shifts focus away from personal worries and cultivates a more positive outlook.
- Improved Mental Health: Regular engagement in contribution activities is associated with improved mental health outcomes, including lower rates of depression and enhanced resilience in coping with life's challenges.

1. Development of Empathy and Compassion:

- Expanded Perspective: Contributing exposes individuals to diverse experiences and perspectives, fostering empathy and understanding for others' circumstances and challenges.
- Cultivation of Compassion: Acts of contribution nurture compassionate responses to the needs and struggles of others, promoting a more caring and empathetic approach to interpersonal relationships and societal issues.

1. Sense of Empowerment and Agency:

- Active Citizenship: Contributing empowers individuals to take an active role in shaping their communities and society. It provides a platform for advocating for positive change and addressing issues that matter to them.
- Increased Self-Efficacy: Successfully making a difference through contribution reinforces a sense of competence and efficacy. It encourages individuals to believe in their ability to effect positive outcomes in their own lives and the lives of others.

1. Spiritual and Emotional Growth:

- Alignment with Values: Contribution often aligns with personal values and beliefs, promoting spiritual growth and deepening one's

sense of identity and purpose.
- Emotional Resonance: Acts of contribution evoke positive emotions such as joy, gratitude, and satisfaction, contributing to emotional well-being and a sense of spiritual fulfillment.

1. Legacy and Long-Term Impact:

- Building a Legacy: Contribution allows individuals to leave a positive impact on future generations and create a lasting legacy of kindness, compassion, and social responsibility.
- Sustainable Change: Engaging in contribution efforts that address systemic issues and promote sustainable practices contributes to long-term societal change and environmental stewardship.

Ways to Contribute

1. Service to Others: Engaging in acts of service is a direct way to contribute to the well-being of others and the community. This can range from volunteering at local organizations, helping neighbors in need, or participating in community clean-up efforts. Service not only benefits those receiving assistance but also fosters a sense of fulfillment and purpose in the giver.
2. Sharing Knowledge and Skills: Each person possesses unique talents and skills that can be shared with others. Teaching or mentoring individuals who can benefit from your expertise—whether in academic subjects, professional skills, or creative arts—provides invaluable support and empowerment. Consider offering workshops, tutoring sessions, or online courses to share your knowledge widely.
3. Supporting Causes and Movements: Contributing to causes you believe in—such as environmental conservation, social justice, or healthcare initiatives—can make a significant impact. This may involve donating money, fundraising, participating in advocacy campaigns, or volunteering time to raise awareness and support for these issues.
4. Emotional and Spiritual Support: Offering emotional support to

friends, family, or strangers going through challenging times is a powerful form of contribution. Simply listening with empathy, providing encouragement, or offering a comforting presence can make a meaningful difference in someone's life. Spiritual support, such as offering prayers, positive intentions, or meditative practices for others, can also be deeply impactful.

5. Creativity and Artistic Expression: Art has the ability to inspire, provoke thought, and uplift spirits. Contributing through artistic expression—whether through visual arts, music, writing, or performance—allows you to share your perspective, evoke emotions, and foster connection with audiences. Consider creating art that promotes positivity, social change, or spiritual reflection.
6. Environmental Stewardship: Taking care of the planet is a vital form of contribution. Practices such as reducing waste, conserving energy and water, supporting sustainable products, and participating in local conservation efforts contribute to environmental stewardship. Educating others about eco-friendly practices can also amplify your impact.
7. Acts of Kindness: Simple acts of kindness—such as holding the door open for someone, offering a smile, or giving a compliment—can brighten someone's day and create a ripple effect of positivity. These small gestures can significantly improve someone's mood and sense of connection, demonstrating that even small actions can have a big impact.
8. Supporting Local Businesses and Communities: Contributing to local economies by supporting small businesses, artisans, and local initiatives helps sustain community vibrancy and economic resilience. Whether through patronage, word-of-mouth support, or collaborative projects, investing in local communities fosters a sense of belonging and mutual support.
9. Advocating for Change: Speaking out against injustice, inequality, or systemic issues is a powerful form of contribution. This may involve participating in peaceful protests, signing petitions, writing letters to policymakers, or advocating for policy changes that promote fairness and equality. Your voice and actions can contribute to creating a more

just and compassionate society.
10. Cultivating Compassion and Empathy: Developing a compassionate mindset and practicing empathy in daily interactions with others promotes understanding, tolerance, and unity.

By exploring these diverse ways to contribute, individuals can discover meaningful avenues to make a positive impact in their communities and beyond, fostering personal growth, fulfillment, and spiritual enrichment along the way.

Reflective Exercise:

1. Personal Contribution Inventory

Take a moment to list all the ways you currently contribute to others and your community, whether through volunteering, supporting loved ones, or advocating for causes. Reflect on how these contributions make you feel and the impact they have on those around you.

1. Exploring Barriers and Strategies

Identify any barriers or challenges that have prevented you from contributing as much as you'd like. Reflect on possible strategies that could help overcome these barriers. Write down actionable steps you can take to start or increase your contributions.

1. Impact Assessment

Choose a recent contribution or act of kindness you've performed. Reflect on the impact it had on others and yourself. How did it align with your values and goals? Consider ways to amplify or expand the positive impact of similar actions in the future.

1. Vision for Contribution

Imagine your ideal vision of how you would like to contribute to the world. Visualize the specific actions you would take and the kind of impact you would like to have. Write a letter to yourself describing this vision and the steps you will take to bring it to fruition.

1. Future Commitments

Set specific, achievable goals for future contributions. Reflect on why these goals are meaningful to you and how they align with your personal values and aspirations. Write an action plan outlining steps, timelines, and resources needed to achieve these goals.

"Success must include two things: the development of an individual to his utmost potentiality and a contribution of some kind to one's world."
– Eleanor Roosevelt

Chapter Nineteen: Explore Your Creativity

Being creative comes naturally to me. It is in my DNA, my heart, and my soul. I remember as a young child watching the CBC television show Mr. Dressup. Mr. Dressup would create unique things for us to do at home. Although my mother did not engage with me, I remember being creative despite my roadblocks. I remember making Barbie doll clothes out of my pillowcases when I was in grade one, though that didn't go over very well with my parents. I thought I was being resourceful by utilizing DIY (do it yourself) projects. I also remember using an old cardboard box and turning it into a board game, complete with pieces. My friend and I designed the game, complete with all the rules. In school, I excelled in arts and crafts but struggled with academic courses. My heart sang when I was allowed to express my creativity.

I have always had an artistic side and find it fascinating. When I was in high school, I went to a very small country school that did not offer any art courses, so I had to take it by correspondence, which was not the same at all. It was terrible, to tell you the truth—it did not feed my creative juices at all. After high school, I studied art at a local college—not extensively, but just enough to feed my soul's inspirations. This background helps me appreciate the wide array of creative activities around me. I fed my creative spirit by doing hair and makeup for my career.

I know, however, what it is like to lose your creative spark. After the trauma I endured during *Soul Dance*, even writing was a challenge. It seemed that I had lost all my creative energy. That is one of the main reasons why it took me so long to write the book—the loss of my creativity and my brain health issues. These days, I am slowly getting my groove back. I find myself surrounded by creative people and fuel my creative spirit with writing—like writing this book, for instance. I also love to write poetry; it speaks to me on a deep soul level.

I am blessed to be on Vancouver Island, which is full of creative people. Susan, my roommate, is an amazing artist who inspires me to be more creative. Gary is both an artist and a musician, channeling his creativity in multiple ways. I have a friend who makes beautiful jewelry, and Amy often does arts and crafts with her friend online.

Creativity is an essential component of a passionate and fulfilling life. It is not just about creating art, writing, or music; it is about tapping into the depths of your imagination and allowing your inner self to be expressed in unique and meaningful ways. Engaging in creative activities can be a powerful tool for personal growth, emotional healing, and spiritual awakening. When we allow ourselves to explore our creativity, we open doors to new possibilities, ideas, and perspectives that enrich our lives.

Living on less does not mean living without joy or passion. In fact, it can be an opportunity to discover and cultivate your creative potential. By embracing creativity, you can transform everyday experiences into extraordinary moments, making life more vibrant and meaningful. Whether you are painting a picture, writing a poem, playing an instrument, or simply brainstorming new ideas, creativity can help you connect with your true self and the world around you.

Being creative is a powerful way to raise your vibration and move closer to your goals, both spiritually and physically. It boosts your happiness and doesn't need to cost much to get started. Creativity isn't limited to a paintbrush and canvas, though that's wonderful if it's your passion. It involves the use of imagination and original thinking to produce something novel and valuable. Creativity is not confined to the arts; it can be found in science, business, technology, and everyday problem solving. It is about seeing the world in new ways. Whether through artistic expression, inventive problem solving, or innovative thinking, creativity allows individuals to bring forth unique contributions to the world.

Creativity plays a crucial role in both personal and spiritual growth. On a personal level, engaging in creative activities helps individuals explore their inner world, discover their passions, and develop a sense of self. It fosters self-expression, enabling people to communicate their thoughts, feelings, and experiences in ways that words alone may not capture. This process of self-discovery and expression is essential for personal growth, as it helps individuals understand themselves better and builds confidence in their abilities.

From a spiritual perspective, creativity is a means of connecting with the divine or the higher self. It allows individuals to tap into a deeper source of inspiration and wisdom, often leading to moments of insight and enlightenment. Creative practices such as art, music, and writing can serve as meditative activities which quiet the mind and open the heart, facilitating a connection to one's spiritual essence. By nurturing creativity, individuals can experience a greater sense of purpose and fulfillment, as they align their actions with their innermost values and aspirations.

Creativity comes in many forms, each offering unique ways to express yourself and explore new ideas. Here are some common forms of creativity:

1. **Visual Arts**:

- Painting
- Drawing
- Sculpture
- Photography
- Graphic Design

1. **Performing Arts**:

- Dance
- Theatre
- Singing
- Composing
- Playing musical instruments
- Acting
- Stand-up Comedy

1. **Writing and Literature**:

- Fiction
- Non-fiction
- Poetry
- Journaling
- Screenwriting
- Storytelling

1. **Crafts and DIY**:

- Knitting and Crocheting
- Sewing
- Quilting
- Woodworking
- Jewelry Making

1. **Culinary Arts:**

- Cooking
- Baking
- Food Presentation
- Mixology (cocktail making)

1. **Digital Creativity:**

- Digital art
- Video editing
- Animation
- Web design
- Game design

1. **Home and Garden:**

- Interior design
- Gardening
- Landscaping
- DIY home improvement projects

1. **Problem-Solving and Innovation:**

- Scientific research
- Engineering
- Product design
- Business solutions
- Marketing strategies

SOULFUL MINIMALISM

1. **Fashion and Style**:

- Clothing design
- Makeup artistry
- Hair styling
- Nail art
- Spa technician
- Accessory design

1. **Hobbies and Leisure Activities**:

- Model building
- Scrapbooking
- Collecting
- Puzzles and brain Teasers

Creativity can be found in almost every aspect of life. It's about finding new ways to approach tasks, solve problems, and express thoughts and emotions. Embracing creativity in various forms can lead to personal growth, joy, and a deeper connection to yourself and the world around you.

Creativity has a profound impact on emotional well-being and happiness. Engaging in creative activities can be a therapeutic process that alleviates stress, anxiety, and depression. When individuals immerse themselves in creative tasks, they enter a state of flow, where time seems to stand still, and they become fully absorbed in the present moment. This state of flow is associated with increased feelings of joy, satisfaction, and inner peace.

By incorporating creativity into daily life, individuals can cultivate a more vibrant and joyful existence, enriched by the continual discovery of new possibilities and expressions of the self.

Creativity and passionate living are intrinsically linked. Creative expression ignites the spark of passion by allowing individuals to explore and manifest their deepest interests and desires. When people engage in creative activities, they tap into a source of inner vitality and enthusiasm that fuels their everyday lives. Whether through painting, writing, playing music, or any other form of artistic endeavor, creativity opens the door to a more vibrant and passionate existence. It encourages individuals to pursue what they love, breaking free from the mundane and the routine, and embracing a life filled with meaning and excitement.

As people explore their creative potential, they uncover hidden talents and passions that might have been suppressed or overlooked. This process of self-discovery fosters a sense of purpose and direction, making life more engaging and fulfilling. By continually nurturing their creative impulses, individuals can maintain a strong connection to their passions, ensuring that they live not just a life of routine, but one of exploration, joy, and profound satisfaction.

Creativity is a powerful tool for living more fully with less. When resources are limited, creativity enables individuals to find innovative solutions and make the most of what they have. It encourages a mindset of abundance rather than scarcity, where the focus is on possibilities and potential rather than limitations. For example, a creative approach to meal planning can turn simple ingredients into delightful dishes, while imaginative home decor ideas can transform a modest space into a cozy, personalized haven.

In times of financial constraints or other challenges, creative thinking can help individuals navigate obstacles and discover new ways to achieve their goals. It promotes resourcefulness, teaching people to repurpose and reinvent rather than discard and replace. This not only conserves resources but also instills a sense of accomplishment and pride in one's ability to thrive despite limitations.

Unleashing your creative potential begins with identifying your unique interests and passions. Creativity is a deeply personal experience, and it flourishes when you engage in activities that genuinely resonate with you. Start by reflecting on what excites you and makes you feel alive. Consider the activities that you naturally gravitate towards, whether it's painting, writing, cooking, gardening, music, or any other form of creative expression. Pay attention to the moments when you lose track of time because you are so absorbed in what you're doing—these are often clues to your true passions.

Take time to explore different creative outlets without judgment or pressure to excel. Experiment with new hobbies and revisit activities you enjoyed as a child. Allow yourself the freedom to play and be curious. Journaling can also be a helpful tool for self-discovery. Write about your dreams, interests, and the creative pursuits you've always wanted to try. By listening to your inner voice and honoring your genuine interests, you can begin to uncover the creative passions that will bring joy and fulfillment to your life.

Once you have identified your creative interests, the next step is to take practical actions to bring them into your daily life. Start small and build gradually to avoid feeling overwhelmed. Set aside a specific time each day or week dedicated to your chosen creative activity. Consistency is key to developing your skills and maintaining your enthusiasm. Create a dedicated space for your creative work, whether it's a corner of a room, a desk, or even a portable setup that you can use as needed.

Don't be afraid to seek inspiration and guidance from others. Join local or online communities related to your creative interest. Participate in workshops, classes, or group activities where you can learn from others and share your progress. Surrounding yourself with like-minded individuals can provide motivation and support as you embark on your creative journey.

Creativity is about exploration and self-expression, not perfection. Celebrate your progress, no matter how small, and view mistakes as opportunities for growth and learning. Be patient with yourself and enjoy the journey of discovering and nurturing your creative potential. By taking these practical steps, you can cultivate a fulfilling and passionate life enriched by the joy of creative expression.

Engaging in creative activities doesn't have to break the bank. Many affordable materials and resources are available for those looking to explore their creativity on a budget. Begin by seeking out basic supplies such as paper, pencils, and paints, which can often be found at dollar stores or discount retailers. Thrift stores and garage sales are treasure troves for finding inexpensive materials, from fabric scraps to old books and magazines that can be repurposed for collage and mixed media projects.

Additionally, online platforms such as Freecycle, Craigslist, and Facebook Marketplace offer free or low-cost items that people are giving away. Libraries and community centers may also provide access to art supplies and tools that can be borrowed or used on-site. By being resourceful and creative in sourcing materials, you can embark on various artistic endeavors without straining your budget.

DIY and upcycling projects are fantastic ways to utilize what you already have at home while reducing waste and saving money. Everyday household items can be transformed into unique art supplies. For instance, old newspapers and magazines can be used for collage and decoupage, while cardboard boxes and packaging materials can be repurposed for sculptures or models. Glass jars and containers can be turned into paintbrush holders or storage for small craft supplies.

Upcycling is about giving new life to items that might otherwise be discarded. Fabric from old clothes can be used for sewing projects, and leftover yarn can be turned into colorful weaving or knitting projects. Nature also provides abundant free materials—leaves, twigs, and stones can be incorporated into various artistic creations. Embracing DIY and upcycling not only saves money but also encourages a sustainable approach to creativity.

Connecting with creative communities and participating in workshops can greatly enhance your artistic journey, and many of these opportunities are available for free or at low cost. Local community centers, libraries, and nonprofit organizations often host free or affordable art classes and workshops. These settings provide a supportive environment to learn new skills and meet like-minded individuals.

Online platforms like Meetup, Eventbrite, and social media groups are excellent resources for finding creative events and workshops. Many artists and creators offer free tutorials and classes on YouTube and other online learning platforms, allowing you to learn new techniques from the comfort of your home. Additionally, joining online forums and communities dedicated to your particular interest can provide inspiration, feedback, and support.

By tapping into these resources, you can immerse yourself in a vibrant creative community without significant financial investment. These connections and learning opportunities can be instrumental in nurturing your creative passions and fostering a sense of belonging and inspiration.

Reflective Exercises:
1: Musical Inspirations

- Choose a piece of music that resonates with you on a deep soul level. What kind of music makes you want to get up and dance? What type of music do you want to start to create your next masterpiece in the

reflective exercises below.
- Spend time listening mindfully. Pay attention to the emotions and thoughts that arise.

2: Create a Picture of Your True Soul Self

- Gather Your Supplies: Find some art materials that inspire you, such as colored pencils, crayons, paints, or markers. Choose a larger piece of art paper (at least 8x10 inches) to give yourself plenty of space to explore.

- Begin Your Creative Journey: Set aside a quiet, comfortable space where you can focus on your art. This exercise is not about creating a traditional self-portrait but about expressing your true soul self in a way that resonates deeply with you.

- Tap into Your Inner Child: Allow yourself to have fun with this project. Imagine what your soul would look like if it were a vivid, colorful creation. Don't worry about accuracy or realism—this is about capturing the essence of who you are at the core.

- Express Your True Self: As you draw or paint, think about the qualities, emotions, and aspirations that make up your true self. Use colors, shapes, and symbols that feel right to you. Let your intuition guide you in creating a piece that feels authentic and meaningful.

- Reflect on Your Creation: After you've finished your artwork, take a moment to reflect on what you've created. What does your soul self look like? How do the colors, shapes, and symbols you chose represent your inner self? Write down your thoughts and feelings about the process and the finished piece.

- Engage with Your Inner Child: Remember, this exercise is a playful exploration of your inner world. Embrace the freedom to be imaginative and spontaneous. Connecting with your inner child through art can reveal new insights and foster a deeper understanding of yourself.

By engaging in this creative exercise, you can uncover aspects of your soul that might not be immediately visible in your everyday life. Enjoy the process and let your true self shine through your artwork.

3: Write Your Soul Story

- Craft Your Story: With your artwork in front of you, it's time to weave a story that brings your creation to life. Imagine you're writing a fairy tale or a children's book—this is your chance to infuse your narrative with imagination and whimsy. Describe the journey of how and why you created your piece, embracing the artistic flair that your soul's story deserves.

- Explore the Backstory: Begin by setting the scene. Where does your soul's story take place? Is it in a magical land, a fantastical realm, or perhaps within the depths of your own heart? Introduce characters or elements that represent the different facets of your true self. These could be symbolic figures, mythical creatures, or abstract ideas that align with the themes in your artwork.

- Describe the Creation: Share the inspiration behind your art. What emotions, dreams, or aspects of your soul influenced the creation of this piece? Describe the process you went through to bring your vision to life, including any meaningful moments or revelations you experienced along the way.

- Incorporate Artistic Flair: Infuse your story with creative language and vivid imagery. Use descriptive words and imaginative scenarios to captivate the reader and convey the essence of your artwork. Think of how you can turn your story into a delightful, engaging tale that reflects the spirit of your soul.

- Complete the Tale: Ensure your story has a beginning, middle, and end. Conclude with a resolution that ties together the themes and emotions expressed in your artwork. Reflect on what you hope your creation conveys and how it represents your soul's journey.

• Share and Reflect: After writing your soul story, read it aloud or share it with someone close to you. Take note of how the process of writing enhances your understanding of your artwork and your inner self. Use this reflective exercise to deepen your connection with your soul and to celebrate the creative expression that flows from within.

For help with your soul story, consider *Your Soul Dance- A Creative Guided Journal for Memoir Writing*. By writing your soul story, you give voice to the visual representation of your inner self, adding a rich layer of meaning and narrative to your creative expression. Enjoy the process of storytelling and let your imagination guide you as you explore the depths of your soul. By following the guidance and exercises in this chapter, you will learn to embrace and cultivate your creativity, enriching your life with passion and purpose.

"You use a glass mirror to see your face. You use works of art to see your soul."
– George Bernard Shaw

Chapter Twenty: Removing Life's Distractions

I remember when I first decided to move to Vancouver Island. At the time, I was living in a lavish condo in a beautiful part of my hometown. I loved that place—it was spacious, organized, clutter-free, and clean. I'd just gone through an emotional divorce from my common-law husband of 13 years, who always dictated how we decorated. So when I moved out, I decorated the new place entirely by myself, and it was wonderful. I thought I had it all, but there was one thing I didn't have: time. I owned 16 beauty salons and was constantly busy.

That's when I decided to dive into my spiritual path and advance my mediumship abilities. I immersed myself in spiritual studies and became a follower of Esther Hicks from Abraham-Hicks. I've attended her conferences and followed her teachings ever since. One of her teachings involves a 30-day challenge to remove distractions from your life. Inspired by this, I created a book called *Soul Discovery: A 30-Day Process to Awaken Your Soul Self*. While Abraham's approach is different, the essence is the same: gaining a new spiritual outlook on life.

I took Abraham's 30-day challenge while living in my condo. It was glorious. I meditated, only spoke to positive people, listened to music I loved, and read and watched self-help books and videos for 30 days. Those 30 days turned into a year, and soon I became a new person. This process revealed my bipolar disorder. It wasn't all sunshine and roses, but I'm glad I discovered it. Living with bipolar isn't easy, but being aware of it is much better than living a chaotic life without knowing the cause. Mentioning my bipolar disorder is important because it was something that needed "cleaning up" in my life.

Whatever needs clearing will be cleared away. The good will stay, and the negative will fall by the wayside. It can be difficult, but it helped me lead a fulfilling life. My life might be small, and I may have lost a lot due to my brain health issues, but I'm better now as a result of all the clearing. It may seem scary, but I believe in you. I believe that you are strong enough to change your life, no matter the circumstances. I faced many difficulties, but I overcame them. I'm still working my way up, and I can tell you it's fun. I'm having a joyous ride on this journey.

SOULFUL MINIMALISM

However, what I have learned on this journey of life is that social media can become daunting after a while. We get addicted to all the social media sites available today, becoming attached to our phones and never unplugging—hour after hour, day after day. It's something that's become normal in our society. But I can't help but wonder: is this really good for us? It's not much different than watching television shows with commercials. While anything in moderation is fine, we can easily become addicted to the social media phenomenon we have today. Studies show that we are on our phones using social media platforms for an average of 143 minutes per day, per user. Globally, the world spends 720 billion minutes per day using social platforms, according to datareportal.com.

To reduce my activity on social media, I designated specific times to use it, such as during lunch. I also limited the people I followed, choosing based on whether they were positive or negative. I found that very negative posts disrupted my energy for the day, so I unfollowed those types of accounts. Instead, I joined groups and followed pages on Facebook that were positive and uplifting for my soul. This can be a challenge, but I can tell you firsthand that limiting social media is a positive change for your life. It will leave you feeling freer than before and will influence your life in ways that promote positive spiritual growth and personal fulfillment.

In our modern world, distractions are all around us—not just from social media, but from negative people, places, and things that drain our energy and keep us unfocused on our goals. Negative movies and TV shows that don't serve our souls, and various other distractions can pull us away from living a passionate, purpose-driven life. By reducing these distractions, we make room for what truly matters. We create a space where positive energy can flow freely, enhancing our well-being and helping us stay aligned with our true selves.

The 30 Ways in 30 Days Soul Growth Challenge will bring you closer to your goals of living a passionate life. Through this process, you will discover how much lighter and more joyful life can be when you remove the clutter and distractions. You will begin to notice a shift in your energy and a renewed sense of clarity and purpose.

Taking the time to evaluate and limit the distractions in your life is a powerful step toward personal transformation. It requires courage and commitment, but the rewards are immense. You'll find yourself more present, more connected to your inner wisdom, and more capable of creating the life you truly desire.

Remember, this journey is about progress, not perfection. Each small step you take towards reducing distractions and embracing a more mindful way of living brings you closer to a life filled with passion, purpose, and peace. Trust the process, believe in your strength, and know that you have the power to transform your life for the better. As you continue on this path, may you find the freedom, joy, and fulfillment that come from living a life aligned with your highest self. Embrace the journey and let your soul shine.

30 Ways in 30 Days Soul Growth Challenge

1. Turn off your television

- Reduce the noise and distraction from TV. Instead, use this time for activities that nourish your soul, like reading, meditating, or spending time in nature.
- Commit to turning off your television. During this time, observe how your daily routine changes. Notice if you have more time for activities that nourish your soul, such as reading, meditating, or spending time in nature. Reflect in your journal on how the absence of television impacts your mood, productivity, and overall sense of well-being. Write about any new insight or creative ideas that emerge during this period of reduced screen time. Consider if there are any shows or content that you can permanently remove from your viewing habits to maintain this sense of clarity and focus.

2. Limit cell phone use

- Set specific boundaries for your cell phone use, such as no phone usage during meals, in the first hour after waking up, or the last hour before bed. Track your screen time using built-in phone settings or apps, aiming to gradually reduce it each day. Reflect on how limiting your phone use affects your attention span, interpersonal relationships, and mental health. Write about the challenges you face in breaking the habit of constant phone checking and the strategies you used to overcome them. Consider creating a phone-free zone in your home or designating certain hours of the day as technology-free to enhance your focus and mindfulness.

3. Stay off social media

- Take a social media detox. During this time, unfollow or mute accounts that don't bring you joy, inspiration, or positivity. Curate your news feed to include only those people and pages that uplift you. Reflect on how this detox affects your mental and emotional health. Write about any feelings of withdrawal you experience initially and how they change over time. Notice if your self-esteem, mood, or productivity improves as a result of staying off social media. Consider setting long-term social media boundaries, like checking it only once a day or limiting your time spent online.

4. Interact with only high vibrational, easy-going, happy people

- Make a conscious effort to surround yourself with positive, supportive, and high-energy individuals. Reflect on your current social circle and identify which relationships uplift you and which drain your energy. Spend more time with people who inspire and encourage you, and less with those who bring negativity or stress into your life. Write about the changes you notice in your interactions and your overall well-being. Reflect on how these positive connections help you grow spiritually and emotionally. Consider how you can cultivate more such relationships and gently distance yourself from those that do not align with your desired energy.

5. Cancel meetings with other people as much as possible

- Assess your schedule and identify meetings or social engagements that are not essential. Cancel or reschedule these to create more space for self-reflection, relaxation, and personal growth. Use this extra time to engage in activities that bring you joy and peace, such as reading, meditating, or spending time in nature. Reflect on how reducing your social commitments impacts your stress levels and sense of fulfillment. Write about the benefits of having more time for yourself and how it allows you to recharge and focus on your priorities. Consider making it a habit to regularly evaluate and adjust your commitments to maintain a balanced and harmonious lifestyle.

6. Withdraw from society and reality as much as possible

- Withdraw from your usual social and work commitments. Create a personal retreat at home or in nature where you can disconnect from the outside world. During this time, focus on activities that nurture your soul, such as meditation, journaling, reading, or simply being in silence. Reflect on how this period of withdrawal affects your mental clarity and emotional balance. Write about any new insight or revelations that come to you during this time of solitude. Consider incorporating regular mini retreats into your life to maintain your sense of inner peace and connection with your true self.

7. Decide on what is necessary to do and do only that

- Evaluate your daily tasks and responsibilities, identifying which are truly necessary and which can be eliminated or delegated. Focus on completing only the essential tasks that align with your goals and values. Reflect on how this shift in priorities affects your stress level, productivity, and sense of accomplishment. Write about the benefits of simplifying your to-do list and how it frees up time for activities that bring you joy and fulfillment. Consider creating a habit of regularly reassessing your commitments to ensure that you are spending your time and energy on what truly matters to you.

8. Focus on attracting what you want

- Spend time each day visualizing and affirming what you want to attract into your life. Use positive affirmations, vision boards, or meditation to focus your energy on your goals and desires. Reflect on how this practice influences your mindset and actions. Write about any changes you notice in your motivation, opportunities, and overall sense of purpose. Consider how you can incorporate these visualization and affirmation practices into your daily routine to continuously align yourself with your goals and attract the life you desire.

9. Create as much as possible to fire up the passion of your imagination

- Dedicate time each day to engage in creative activities that inspire and energize you, such as painting, writing, crafting, or cooking. Reflect on how these creative pursuits affect your mood and sense of fulfillment. Write about the joy and satisfaction you experience from expressing your creativity. Consider how you can incorporate more creative activities into your life to keep your imagination and passion alive. Reflect on how these creative endeavors help you connect with your inner self and bring more joy and meaning to your daily life.

10. Buy a pretty notebook and journal as much as possible

- Invest in a beautiful notebook. Journal your thoughts, feelings, goals, and experiences. Reflect on how journaling helps you process emotions, gain clarity, and track your personal growth. Write about the insights and revelations that come to you through journaling. Consider setting aside a specific time each day for journaling to make it a regular practice. Reflect on how this dedicated journaling time helps you stay connected to your inner self and supports your soul's journey.

11. Make a list of everything positive in your life. Put it in your journal

- Take time to reflect on all the positive aspects of your life, including your achievements, relationships, experiences, and qualities. Write them down in your journal, along with reasons why you are grateful for each one. Reflect on how this exercise shifts your perspective and enhances your sense of gratitude and appreciation. Write about the positive changes you notice in your mood and outlook on life. Consider making this a regular practice to continuously remind yourself of the abundance and blessings in your life.

12. Meditate daily

- Commit to a daily meditation practice, even if it's just for a few minutes each day. Use guided meditations, mindfulness techniques, or silent meditation to center yourself and connect with your inner peace. Reflect on how regular meditation affects your mental clarity, emotional balance, and overall well-being. Write about any challenges you face in maintaining your practice and the strategies you use to overcome them. Consider how you can integrate meditation into your daily routine to support your soul's growth and maintain a sense of calm and presence.

13. Care about how you feel and record your emotions in your journal

- Pay attention to your emotions throughout the day and take note of how different situations and interactions make you feel. Record your observations in your journal, along with any patterns or triggers you notice. Reflect on how this awareness helps you understand and manage your emotions better. Write about the benefits of being in tune with your feelings and how it supports your emotional and spiritual growth. Consider how you can continue to prioritize your emotional well-being and make choices that align with your true self.

14. Act on impulses! When you are inspired, do it!

- Follow your intuition and act on inspired ideas. This keeps your energy high and aligned with your true self.
- Act on inspired impulses, whether it's starting a new project, reaching out to someone, or trying something new. Reflect on how following your inspiration leads to positive outcomes and growth. Write about

the experiences and opportunities that arise from acting on your impulses. Consider how you can cultivate a habit of listening to and trusting your inner guidance. Reflect on how this practice helps you live more authentically and passionately.

15. Manifestations will start showing up in your life; write them in your journal

- As you focus on your goals and desires, take note of the manifestations and synchronicities that begin to appear in your life. Record these events in your journal, along with your thoughts and feelings about them. Reflect on how these manifestations affirm your ability to attract what you want and reinforce your belief in the power of intention. Write about how these experiences motivate you to continue your practice of visualization and positive thinking. Consider how you can stay open to receiving and recognizing the manifestations that come your way.

16. Start a vision board

- Create a vision board that visually represents your goals, dreams, and desires. Use images, words, and symbols that inspire and motivate you. Place your vision board where you will see it daily. Reflect on how creating and regularly viewing your vision board influences your mindset and actions. Write about the progress you make towards your goals and any new ideas or opportunities which arise. Consider how you can use your vision board as a tool for continuous inspiration and focus on your journey. For guidance, refer to my book on vision boards, *Beyond the Canvas*.

17. Follow people you want to emulate and like, such as people who inspire you

- Identify individuals who embody the qualities, values, and lifestyle you aspire to. Follow their work, read their books, or engage with their content online. Reflect on how these role models influence your mindset and motivate you to grow. Write about the lessons and inspiration you gain from them. Consider how you can incorporate the practices and principles they advocate into your own life. Reflect on how connecting with inspiring people supports your personal and spiritual development.

18. Organize and declutter

- Clear out physical and mental clutter. A tidy space creates a calm mind, making it easier to focus on your soul growth.
- Choose a specific area in your home or life that needs organizing and decluttering. Set aside time to tackle this task, breaking it down into manageable steps. Reflect on the process of decluttering and how it affects your mental clarity and sense of peace. Write about the positive changes you notice in your environment and your mood. Consider how you can maintain a clutter-free space and make organizing a regular habit. Reflect on how a clean and organized environment supports your overall well-being and growth.

19. Appreciate and have gratitude

- Appreciate the small and big things in your life.
- Practice gratitude daily by reflecting on the things, people, and experiences you are grateful for. Write them down in your journal, along with reasons why you appreciate them. Reflect on how focusing on gratitude shifts your perspective and enhances your sense of joy and contentment. Write about the positive changes you notice in your life as a result of cultivating gratitude. Consider how you can make gratitude a regular practice to maintain a positive and abundant mindset.

20. Write about how your energy and vibration are shifting. Record the process in your journal

- Pay attention to the changes in your energy and vibration as you engage in these reflective exercises and practices. Notice how your mood, outlook, and interactions with others evolve. Write about

SOULFUL MINIMALISM

these shifts in your journal, along with any insights or revelations you have. Reflect on the factors that contribute to these positive changes and how you can continue to support your energetic and vibrational growth. Consider how documenting this process helps you to stay connected to your progress and to stay motivated on your journey.

21. Get some form of exercise. Get out in nature—at the very least get some fresh air.

- Incorporate physical activity into your daily routine, whether it's a brisk walk, yoga, or a workout. Spend time outdoors, connecting with nature and breathing in fresh air. Reflect on how regular exercise and time in nature affect your physical health, mood, and energy levels. Write about the benefits you experience from being active and spending time outside. Consider how you can make exercise and nature a regular part of your life to support your overall well-being.

22. Ask Spirit for what you want

- Take time to connect with your higher self, spirit guides, or the universe. Clearly articulate your desires and intentions, asking for guidance and support. Reflect on how this practice influences your mindset and sense of direction. Write about any signs, messages, or manifestations you receive in response to your requests. Consider how you can continue to cultivate a strong connection with spirit and trust in the guidance you receive. Reflect on the sense of peace and empowerment that comes from knowing you are supported on your journey.

23. Stretch your body—try yoga

- Incorporate stretching or yoga into your daily routine to improve flexibility, strength, and relaxation. Choose a time of day that works best for you, whether it's morning, evening, or during breaks. Reflect on how regular stretching or yoga affects your physical and mental well-being. Write about the benefits you experience, such as reduced stress, increased energy, or a greater sense of calm. Consider how you can make stretching or yoga a regular practice to support your overall health and balance.

24. Drink eight glasses of water daily

- Make a conscious effort to drink at least 8 glasses of water each day to stay hydrated and support your body's functions. Track your water intake and reflect on how staying hydrated affects your energy levels, skin, and overall health. Write about any challenges you face in maintaining this habit and the strategies you use to overcome them. Consider how you can make drinking water a regular part of your routine to support your well-being. Reflect on the positive changes you notice as a result of staying properly hydrated.

25. Take care of your nutritional needs

- Plan balanced meals that include a variety of fruits, vegetables, proteins, and whole grains. Reflect on how making healthier food choices affects your energy, mood, and overall well-being. Write about any challenges you face in maintaining a nutritious diet and the strategies you use to overcome them. Consider how you can make healthy eating a regular part of your life to support your physical and mental health.

26. Start a lookbook for inspiration

- Create a lookbook filled with images, quotes, and ideas that inspire you. This can include fashion, home decor, travel destinations, or anything that sparks your creativity and passion. Reflect on how curating a lookbook influences your mindset and motivation. Write about the inspiration and ideas you gain from your lookbook. Consider how you can use it as a tool for continuous inspiration and goal-setting. Reflect on the positive impact of having a visual representation of your dreams and aspirations.

27. Talk to someone you love every day

- Make it a habit to connect with a loved one each day, whether it's through a phone call, video chat, or in-person visit. Reflect on how regular communication with loved ones affects your mood and sense of connection. Write about the benefits of maintaining strong relationships and how they support your emotional and mental well-being. Consider how you can prioritize these connections and make time for meaningful conversations. Reflect on the joy and support you receive from your loved ones and how it enriches your life.

28. Give hugs and receive hugs

- Make physical touch a part of your daily routine by giving and receiving hugs from family, friends, or even pets. Reflect on how physical touch affects your mood, stress levels, and overall sense of connection. Write about the benefits of incorporating more hugs into your life, such as increased feelings of love and support. Consider how you can make hugging a regular practice to enhance your relationships and well-being. Reflect on the warmth and comfort that come from physical touch and how it positively impacts your emotional health.

29. Tell someone you love that you love, care for, and appreciate them

- Express your love, care, and appreciation to someone important in your life each day. Reflect on how sharing these feelings affects your relationships and emotional well-being. Write about the positive changes you notice in your interactions and the sense of fulfillment that comes from expressing your emotions. Consider how you can make this a regular practice to strengthen your connections and bring more positivity into your life. Reflect on the joy and gratitude that come from openly sharing your feelings with others.

30. Watch only inspirational, uplifting movies and talks to inspire you and get your creative juices flowing

- Choose to watch movies, documentaries, and talks that inspire and uplift you. Reflect on how consuming positive and motivational content affects your mindset, creativity, and overall outlook on life. Write about the inspiration and ideas you gain from watching these programs. Consider how you can make it a habit to seek out and consume uplifting content regularly. Reflect on the impact of surrounding yourself with positive influences and how it supports your personal and creative growth.

By incorporating these 30 ways in 30 days, you can cleanse your soul and remove life's distractions, paving the way for deeper spiritual growth and a more fulfilling, passionate life.

Reflective Exercise:

- Start the 30 Ways in 30 Days Challenge
- Journal about your experience

"You can't do big things if you're distracted by small things."
–Unknown

Chapter Twenty-One: Embracing Your Own Unique Life

As we conclude *Soulful Minimalism: 20 Practices for Passionate Living with Less*, it's essential to take a moment to reflect on the journey we've undertaken together. This book was crafted to inspire you to find joy, purpose, and passion in living a life that is not defined by material wealth but by the richness of experiences, connections, and inner fulfillment.

Throughout the chapters, we have delved into various aspects of passionate living—from discovering your soul's blueprint and nurturing supportive relationships to expanding your knowledge and raising your vibration. Each chapter had the aim of providing you with practical tools, reflective exercises, and insights to help you navigate the complexities of living with less while embracing a life full of passion and purpose.

In this final chapter, we will revisit the key themes, offer personal reflections, and provide you with encouragement and practical next steps to continue this journey. Living passionately with less is not a destination but a continuous dance, one that invites you to move with the rhythms of life, finding beauty and meaning in every step.

Living passionately with less is something I discovered after recovering from my brain health issues. On this journey, I have met many interesting people who I would not have encountered if I had been running my beauty empire and driving my lavish SUV, Walter. Now, I take the bus to town. On this local bus that journeys through the countryside to pick people up, you meet individuals like Malcolm, who also lives with a financial disadvantage. Malcolm is a rustic fellow, with holes in his jeans near his backside and an extensively overgrown beard. It was his birthday today, so I kindly said happy birthday to him. He thanked me. My friend Linda, who was also on the bus, asked him what he bought in town that day. Malcolm said he treated himself to potato salad for his birthday. That kind of information has a way of humbling a person. It certainly did for me.

As humans, we collect things—homes, vehicles, books—anything that makes us feel good about ourselves. And there is Malcolm, enjoying his potato salad for his birthday. I say good on you. My birthday is coming up soon, and I will likely celebrate it by writing. If I can afford a $20 bottle of champagne, then I will celebrate with that. A fancy meal is not in the budget, but a $20 bottle of champagne will make me gloriously happy.

In my new life, which comes with its fair share of ups and downs, I find myself happier more often than not. I don't yearn for much, aside from perhaps a bit more money to buy quality groceries like fresh fruits and vegetables. Until then, I take the bus, meet people like Malcolm, and connect with others who can relate to my journey. With my birthday approaching, I've decided not to renew my driver's license. My ego insists I should keep it "just in case," but the humble part of me says to let it go. The $75 renewal fee, plus taxes, is a significant hit to my budget.

This decision takes me back to the days when my father and brother gave me driving lessons. I've had my learner's permit since I was 13, and by 16, I earned my full license. With that license came a used car, marking the beginning of a long road of independence that lasted until I turned 49. Now, I'm content taking the bus wherever I need to go and catching rides from friends when I can. It's a shift that comes with living in poverty, but despite the struggle, I live a happy life.

I hope you have a good life. I hope that you will find a way to live passionately. I know I have. Meeting people like Malcolm makes me appreciate the world in a deeper, more spiritual way. Malcolm is a kind man; my empathy and intuition tell me that. Bless him and the rest of the people I meet on my path through life. People like him make me appreciate my life on a grander scale. I appreciate my disability income and bless my way of life, no matter how modest it is. I also bless people who have more—sometimes just a little more, and sometimes a whole lot more than I have. I bless everyone because we are all on a spiritual journey. Some are aware of it, and some are not. Despite that, I hope people find what they are looking for on their journey through life.

We have explored how to live on less and how to live passionately by finding your faith, setting goals, and discovering your values. Keep journaling and meditating, even if it's only for five minutes a day. These small steps will set you on your path to enlightenment. We have also discussed how to embark on your healing journey, learning to forgive yourself and others along the way. We are now more aware of energy, how it affects us on a spiritual level through intuition, and how it influences the environment in our household. This awareness has guided us toward decluttering and organizing our spaces.

We are closer to finding our soul's purpose, or what some may call the soul's blueprint. We have learned to cultivate gratitude and appreciation for the abundance that surrounds us, regardless of our material circumstances. We have become more mindful of the nourishment we provide to our bodies, both from the outside and within. We have deepened our understanding of compassion and expanded our creativity. Additionally, we have recognized the importance of seeking mentors and continuously educating ourselves.

This is the formula for living a successful life with less. This is *Soulful Minimalism*. This is what your soul desires—for you to be happy no matter what. I urge you to complete the exercises if you haven't already. They will help shift your perspective on life. Each exercise has been carefully designed to facilitate growth, regardless of your current situation. Whether you are financially abundant or not, this journey will help you rediscover your soul.

Living passionately with less is not just a survival tactic but a path to thriving. It's about finding joy in simplicity, embracing the richness of human connection, and cultivating inner peace. The principles and practices shared in this book aim to empower you to live a life of meaning and fulfillment. Remember, your happiness and contentment are not dictated by the abundance of your possessions but by the abundance of your spirit. Embrace this journey with an open heart, and let *Soulful Minimalism* guide you to a life of true passion and purpose.

As you reach the final pages of *Soulful Minimalism*, I want to leave you with words of encouragement and inspiration. Your journey towards living passionately with less is a testament to your courage, resilience, and commitment to a more fulfilling life. Each step you take, no matter how small, is a victory. Remember, the path to self-discovery and transformation is not always easy, but it is always worth it. Embrace each moment, each lesson, and each challenge with an open heart and a determined spirit. Know that you have the power within you to create a life that is rich with meaning, purpose, and joy. You are stronger than you realize, and your potential is limitless.

One of the core messages of this book is that living with less does not mean living without passion or joy. On the contrary, when we strip away the excess and focus on what truly matters, we make room for the things that bring us genuine happiness and fulfillment. Simplifying your life allows you to connect more deeply with your passions, whether they be creative pursuits, meaningful relationships, or personal growth. It frees you from the distractions and burdens of materialism, enabling you to live more authentically and with greater intention. Remember, a life lived with passion and joy is not determined by what you have, but by who you are and how you choose to live each day.

As you navigate this journey, it is essential to practice self-compassion and patience. Change does not happen overnight, and there will be times when you may feel overwhelmed or discouraged. Be gentle with yourself during these moments. Acknowledge your efforts and celebrate your progress, no matter how small it may seem. Understand that self-improvement is a lifelong process, and it is okay to take it one step at a time. Treat yourself with the same kindness and understanding that you would offer a dear friend. By cultivating self-compassion and patience, you create a supportive environment for growth and transformation, allowing yourself the grace to flourish at your own pace.

As we conclude this journey together, I hope that *Soulful Minimalism* has inspired you to embrace a life of passion, purpose, and simplicity. May you find joy in the little things, strength in your challenges, and peace in your journey. Remember, you have the power to create a beautiful and meaningful life, no matter the circumstances. Dance under the moonlight with your soul, and let your inner light guide you. Thank you for sharing this journey with me, and may your path be filled with endless love, light, and fulfillment.

As you move forward, remember that the journey to passionate living is ongoing. Embrace the process with an open heart and a resilient spirit. Each day presents an opportunity to live authentically, align with your values, and pursue your passions. Thank you for allowing *Soulful Minimalism* to be a part of your journey. May you continue to dance under the moonlight with joy, purpose, and a soul full of light.

• • • •

Moon Dance

I find you in the air, the wind, the sea.
You appear in my dreams, my heart, my soul.
I have only my suitcase and inspirations,

SOULFUL MINIMALISM

Yet you are with me in spirit, leading the way.
I hold dear only my heart and memories within.
Life's essentials burden me as I carry them by my side.
Walking along my soul's road, paved with yellow bricks,
I walk alone, with only Spirit as my guide.
New faces come; some stay, some leave.
In the mirror, I see the only familiar face.
This lonely road can destroy you if you let it,
But I have the Great Spirit by my side.
Money is scarce, but abundance is within.
I am rich in life's harvest,
Finding my soul beneath the moonlight as I dance—
A priceless treasure no money can buy.
Escaping life's traumas with my soul intact,
I complete the soul dance journey.
Now I know the road never ends;
The key is to continue with gratitude for what you have.
The universe is real, present for you.
Look in the mirror—the universe is you.
Once you recognize your power,
The secret is to find joy in all that you have.
by Karen Rose Kobylka

KAREN ROSE KOBYLKA

"Underneath a full moon, as you dance, you are reminded that beauty exists in the simplest of things."
—Karen Rose Kobylka

Recommended Reading

Soul Dance By Karen Rose Kobylka
The Beauty Empire By Karen Rose Kobylka
Your Soul Dance By Karen Rose Kobylka
Beyond The Canvas By Karen Rose Kobylka
Soul Discovery By Karen Rose Kobylka
Spiritual Insights Journal By Karen Rose Kobylka
Blossoming Intuition By Karen Rose Kobylka
Awakened Creativity By Karen Rose Kobylka
Manifesting Miracles By Karen Rose Kobylka
Soulful Reflections By Karen Rose Kobylka
Seeds of Thanks By Karen Rose Kobylka
The Myth of Normal: Trauma, Illness and Healing in a Toxic Culture by Gabor Maté MD, Daniel Maté
Healing with words, Kaur (guided prompt journal)
The Anatomy of Loneliness: How to Find Your Way Back to Connection By Teal Swan
Raise Your Vibration, By Kyle Gray
Soul Coaching By Denise Linn
The Law of Attraction By Esther and Jerry Hicks
The Artist's Way By Julia Cameron
Ask and it is Given By Esther and Jerry Hicks
The Seat of the Soul By Gary Zukav
Life Visioning By Michael Bernard Beckwith
The Tao Te Ching 101: A Modern, Practical Guide, Plain and Simple By Matthew Barnes
Trust Your Vibes By Sonia Choquette

References

Chapter One-
https://resetyourfinance.com/money-mindfulness-and-you-why-financial-self-care-is-essential/
https://techbullion.com/do-financial-advisers-help-with-retirement-planning//
https://apartmentprepper.com/smart-shopping-how-to-save-money-on-groceries-without-couponing//
https://medium.com/@mealfave/dinnertime-made-easy-pre-schedule-your-family-meals-for-a-relaxing-evening-2d13c257c8cd
https://workweeklunch.com/meal-planning-for-intuitive-eating/

Chapter Three-
https://mindfulnessvalley.com/message-from-the-universe/the-power-of-forgiveness//
https://www.flatironschurch.com/sermon/forgiveness—week-2/[1]

Chapter Four-
The Artist's Way by Julia Cameron.
https://gracemastered.com/journaling-ideas/

Chapter Six-
https://www.linkedin.com/pulse/psychological-impact-interior-design-nexencyp-ausoe
https://www.minimalismmadesimple.com/home/zen-of-delcuttering/

Chapter Seven-
https://www.lifehack.org/568438/what-toxic-relationship-and-how-deal-with/
https://www.classace.io/answers/discuss-how-positive-relationships
https://www.psychowellnesscenter.com/Blog/5-steps-to-give-yourself-permission-to-let-go-of-a-friendship

Chapter Fourteen-
https://beingkind.com/

Chapter Fifteen-
https://jeanettebrown.net/the-art-of-being-grateful-9-ways-to-cultivate-a-thankful-mindset//[2]

Chapter Sixteen-
Apples: https://dealiciousness.net/traditional-apple-butter-recipe//

Chapter Twenty-
Esther Hicks/Abraham hicks- 30-day challenge

---

1. https://www.flatironschurch.com/sermon/forgiveness--week-2/
2. https://jeanettebrown.net/the-art-of-being-grateful-9-ways-to-cultivate-a-thankful-mindset/

Acknowledgements

Thank you to Amy my bestie and editor.

Meet Karen Rose Kobylka

From a very young age, I felt the gentle tug of the spiritual realm, a calling that whispered to me throughout my life. For years, I kept this profound connection to the spiritual world hidden, sharing it only with my beloved mother, who has since passed. You see, I defy the conventional image of a spiritual medium. Grounded in logic, observation, and a deep sense of practicality, I may appear to be just like anyone else you know. However, there's more of me waiting to be discovered.

Since childhood, I have possessed the remarkable ability to see and communicate with spirits. It's a gift that I've carried with me, quietly and discreetly, shying away from the stereotypes perpetuated by the media and popular culture. However, a decade ago, I decided it was time to embrace my true self and share my talents with the world.

Today, I proudly offer readings on occasion at a local gift shop, where I harness my intuition and mediumship skills to help you uncover the answers you seek. If you can't visit in person, I'm also available for online readings at www.karenrosekobylka.com[1].

Beyond my role as a spiritual medium, I am working on providing spiritual consultations. Drawing on my training as a Law of Attraction and spiritual life coach, I am dedicated to helping people heal and navigate the crossroads of life. We often seek guidance when faced with life's complexities, and I'm here to provide that guidance.

I am a professionally trained intuitive, an evolving evidential spiritual medium, and a trance healer. When you receive an intuitive reading from me, you can trust that the wisdom and insights I share come directly from the spirit world. As an all-senses medium, I utilize my intuition to guide all my clients, empowering them to move forward with positivity and confront the challenges that await them.

My journey as a medium has been enriched by the teachings of esteemed mentors, some of whom have imparted their wisdom at the renowned Arthur Findley College in England. I've been professionally trained to provide

---

1. http://www.karenrosekobylka.com

evidential mediumship, ensuring that the messages I convey are not just meaningful but also deeply authentic.

My life's purpose has always been crystal clear: to help people. Whether through my intuitive readings, spiritual consultations, or healing sessions, my mission is to be a beacon of guidance and healing, illuminating the path for those who seek it.

Thank you for joining me on this journey through *Soulful Minimalism: Living Passionately with Less*. I hope the insights and practices shared in this book inspire you to find joy, passion, and fulfillment in every aspect of your life, no matter your circumstances.

For more of my books scan me:

For more of my Journals & books scan me:

Coming Winter of 2024/2025

Don't miss out!

Visit the website below and you can sign up to receive emails whenever Karen Rose Kobylka publishes a new book. There's no charge and no obligation.

https://books2read.com/r/B-A-NOWDB-HLHZE

BOOKS 2 READ

Connecting independent readers to independent writers.

Did you love *Soulful Minimalism*? Then you should read *Soul Dance*[2] by Karen Rose Kobylka!

A Medium's Triumph Over Bipolar Disorder, Mania, Psychosis And Betrayal

Step into the rhythm of your soul's journey with 'Soul Dance', the inspiring memoir of a spiritual medium's triumph over bipolar disorder, mania, psychosis and betrayal, and the rediscovery of her path through the healing power of spirit. The souls speak, dance, and arrive in Soul Dance. It is a true story which was written by spiritual medium Karen Rose Kobylka. This is a story of hope which rises from tragedy, rape, addiction, suicide, loss, mania, and psychosis. As Karen's mental health fails, she goes on a journey with Spirit that takes her deep beneath the depths of her soul. Karen was faced with homelessness, poverty and jail after a spiritual church charges her with criminal harassment. This once beauty business mogul loses everything, then Spirit intervenes and helps Karen to connect to life on a deeper level. Soul Dance is a book on how

---

2. https://books2read.com/u/3RwD5j

3. https://books2read.com/u/3RwD5j

Karen recovered from trauma on a soul level. It will show the reader how Karen faced her challenges and started to heal her life. Karen speaks to souls, and they speak back through trance mediumship. Follow her and her Collective Souls in this inspired journey of self-discovery.

Read more at https://www.karenrosekobylka.com.

Also by Karen Rose Kobylka

Soul Dance
Soulful Minimalism

Watch for more at https://www.karenrosekobylka.com.

www.ingramcontent.com/pod-product-compliance
Lightning Source LLC
Chambersburg PA
CBHW030234170426
43201CB00006B/210